LEARN
JUST ENOUGH
— *to* —
GET LAID

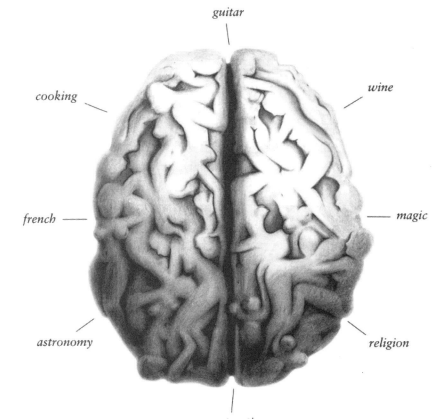

guitar

cooking

wine

french

magic

astronomy

religion

construction

Tyler DeAngelo & Brad Emmett

Illustrated by Kendra Malcolm

Published by Seven Footer Press
247 West 30th Street, 11th Floor
New York, NY. 10001

First Printing, December 2010
10 9 8 7 6 5 4 3 2

Illustrated by Kendra Malcolm

ISBN-13 978-1-934734-90-2

www.learnjustenoughtogetlaid.com
www.sevenfooterpress.com

Contents

Learn Just Enough...

to Get Laid

"Girls only want boyfriends who have great skills."

—Napoleon Dynamite

Why This Book Isn't for Dummies or Idiots

Bookstores are well-stocked with condescending how-to guides with titles like *The Illiterate Circus Freak's Guide to Classical Ballet* and *Advanced Astrophysics for Morons*.

You're merely trying to learn a skill. Why are these publishers being so hurtful? By the time you've read one of these abusive volumes, you may have successfully learned your desired skill, but now you feel completely worthless. "Well, I guess I can play the accordion now. Too bad I'm still an idiot."

You're not an idiot. Okay, you probably are, but we can't prove it, and frankly we don't care. Our goal is not to ridicule you. We're merely attempting to teach you a portfolio's worth of impressive skills in as short a time as humanly possible. This means cutting out all the minutiae, condensing all the repetition—and avoiding the truly difficult parts all together. With a minimal investment of time and money, we can give you the appearance of mastery with almost none of the effort.

That's right. We're not here to make you an expert at anything. Nor is this a beginner's guide—because that would imply you're going to continue developing these skills. In our opinion, that won't be necessary. The law of diminishing returns stipulates that there's a sweet spot in how much time you should invest into something before the rewards begin to taper off.

And when we say "rewards," we're not talking about some sort of abstract spiritual satisfaction. We have no idea how one would even begin to obtain such a thing. Instead, we've carefully assembled a catalogue of easy-to-learn subjects that have been repeatedly proven to do one thing above all else: attract women.

By the end of each of our eight chapters, you will have just the tentative grasp of a skill you need to impress girls. Our format is simple. We're going to tell you what materials you'll need and how much time it'll take, and then we'll distill the essential information into a series of easy-to-follow instructions. Reading through one of our chapters will be like the first time you had sex: It'll be over quickly, you'll have your hand held the entire time, and by the end of it, we'll both be crying.

Just remember that the results don't need to stand the test of time—they simply need to stand the test of the time it takes for a girl to sleep with you.

We only ask that you avoid putting more work into this book than is required. Pick and choose our chapters. Skim our sidebars. Look at our pictures. Gloss over our steps. If something seems too difficult, skip over it entirely. In other words, don't read this book cover to cover. Just read enough of it to get laid.

Before You Score

We're pretty confident that you've already mastered how to oper-
ate a regular book. And based on the fact that you're mentally
processing this paragraph, we can only assume that you're fully
literate. Still, there are a few features of *Learn Just Enough* that
make it stand out, and they require a little explanation.

Learn Just Enough About VideoMarks

Browsing *Learn Just Enough*, the first thing you'll probably ask
yourself is, "What the hell are those bar-code-looking things? I'm
trying to get laid, not solve the fucking Da Vinci Code."

We call them VideoMarks. They are designed to link static written
instructions with easy-to-follow video tutorials that play instantly
on your mobile phone. VideoMarks appear throughout the book
whenever we feel words alone just aren't enough.

Like everything else in this book, we've made using VideoMarks as
easy as possible. If you've got your phone handy, you're ready to go.

1. You'll first need to install a free QR code reader onto your
phone. We personally use ScanLife, and it works great. To down-
load ScanLife, simply search for it in your app store or go to
getscanlife.com using your mobile phone's browser. Alternatively,
you can text "SCAN" to 43588.

2. Launch your code reader application and follow the instructions to scan a VideoMark.

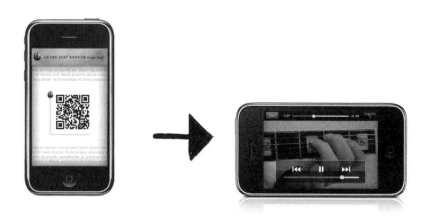

3. That's it. Once a VideoMark is scanned, the associated video or picture will appear on your phone.

You can practice on the VideoMark below.

VideoMark:
Why Women Like
Guys with Skills

Disclaimer: Standard data rates may apply.

Learn Just Enough About Our Structure

Our chapters are divided into five distinct sections, each corresponding to a different level of instruction. To keep the pace brisk, we designed the book so that you'll unearth a valuable nugget of information every step of the way.

Introduction: To get you and the subject matter a little better acquainted, we've included brief introductions. They're kind of like a round of drinks before a meal—something to get you in the right frame of mind. We use this opportunity to explain why we've selected the chapter's skill and to spell out everything you can expect to learn from our instruction.

Not Quite Enough: Here we dive headfirst into the shallow end of the pool with a very basic lesson—for example, how to properly hold a guitar. Think of this section like foreplay: It may or may not be absolutely required, but it'll definitely help ensure success when the important stuff comes up.

Almost Enough: Before you enjoy the fruits of your labor, you'll first need to learn some essential material that's directly related to the chapter skill. This is where we include all of your final preparations.

Just Enough: Here it is, what we've been leading up to this whole time. This is the climax, the part we all wish we could skip ahead to. In our guitar chapter, we teach you the actual music; in cooking, the actual recipes. This is where we equip you with exactly what you need to seal the deal.

A Sure Thing: This is the *coup de grace*. At this point, we are confident you know enough to get laid. This section is to keep her coming back for more.

Learn Just Enough About Our Sidebars

We've done the trial and error for you. Scattered throughout the chapter, we'll be including supplementary advice and forewarnings so that you get the most out of our lesson plans and avoid wasting any unnecessary time.

 Anatomy Lesson: Using illustrated diagrams, we dissect any major objects you'll need. That way you won't have to waste time dissecting them yourself using power tools and fire.

 The Bare Necessities: So you're fully prepared, we list a few things you'll need to complete each chapter before you even begin. Think of it as an insultingly easy scavenger hunt.

 Blue Balls Beware: Murphy's Law states that if something can go wrong, it will go wrong. We help you steer clear of the many foibles and frustrations that can ruin a date and cause an unhealthy fluid buildup in your nard area.

 On Good Terms: We provide you with terms that are not only important to know for the sake of learning your skill, but also great to casually drop into conversation. That way, you can at least make it seem like you know what you're talking about.

 Just the Tip: Occasionally, we'll provide short, penetrative tips, so you can work your way through our lessons with a clear head.

View from a Broad: We go directly to the source and get actual girls to explain why the skills we're teaching you are so damn sexy.

Quintessential Quotation: When something's been said before we had a chance to say it ourselves, we give due credit. Our copyright lawyers refuse to let us just steal the material.

Guitar

Not Quite Enough — Holding Your Instrument

Almost Enough — Playing Chords

Just Enough — Playing Songs

A Sure Thing — Writing Your Own Music

*F*emale fascination with guitar players is one of life's cruelest double standards. Whereas dudes that play most stringed instruments (violin, cello, harp) get their asses kicked, dudes that play guitar (acoustic, double neck, flying V) get their asses laid. A lot.

The appeal comes from the guitar's dual cultural connotations. It is simultaneously a symbol of counterculture rebellion and a means to convey profound emotional sensitivity. Even the sturdiest of female constitutions melts when faced with this contradiction. If these women could only get past your thin eggshell of external edginess, perhaps they would find that loving soul they thought they heard in your music.

Of course, there's a reason you haven't learned the guitar already: it's an intimidating instrument. Watching a skilled guitarist's unfathomable dexterity is reason enough to never bother, as these people have clearly spent a lifetime honing their obnoxious abilities. The amount of work implicit in this is preposterous, doubtless requiring years of hard work—perhaps even a dedication to celibacy. Meanwhile, you've probably dedicated these same years to celibacy entirely by accident and have nothing to show for it. And at this point, you don't exactly have a lifetime at your disposal to sit around learning the guitar.

The good news is that we can circumvent all the hard work. Give us 10 minutes for every decade these guitar masters spent practicing and you'll reap many of the same rewards. By the end of this chapter, you should be able to play the most recognizable parts of a couple popular tunes and vaguely declare that you're in the process of writing a song of your own.

You might be left wondering: "But won't I need to shred wicked guitar solos to impress girls? I'm not capable of that." Of course you're not. Listen, girls don't care how well you play. They just want to sing along to songs they know—and to brag to their jealous friends that the Adonis who took them to unimaginable sexual heights (that's you, BTW) is a musician.

But let's stop worrying about the "why" and focus on the "how." We'll be your sensei in this ancient art that's gotten greasy-haired, ugly-ass guys laid for years. We won't sweat the details. We're focused on teaching you just enough material to strum coherently by Saturday night.

According to our lawyers, we can't legally guarantee this will get you laid. But off the record, these same lawyers told us you can probably expect at least a handjob.

The Bare Necessities

Six-string acoustic guitar, comfortable chair, condoms, unkempt facial hair, false sense of entitlement.

If you are unable to borrow a friend's acoustic guitar, Craigslist or pawnshops are good places to start. Note: These same resources can be used to meet girls after you've completed this chapter.

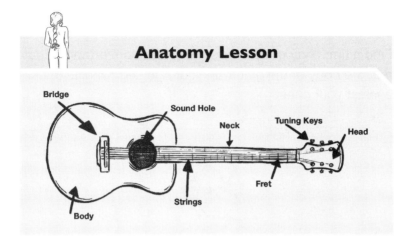

Anatomy Lesson

Bridge

Sound Hole

Neck

Tuning Keys

Head

Fret

Strings

Body

Part of the appeal of guitar players comes from the sheer attractiveness of the guitar itself. The standard acoustic guitar is an elegant embodiment of form and function. Even if you're incapable of strumming a note, holding a guitar is like having a little midget wingman sitting right in your lap.

We recommend against an electric guitar. While we understand the temptation to re-create the celebrated "Enchantment Under the Sea" scene in *Back to the Future*, the production of dragging out an amplifier and wailing a few bars of "Johnny Be Good" into a girl's face is neither practical nor suggestive of intimacy.

Not Quite Enough — Holding Your Instrument

For the amateur, holding a guitar for the first time will feel a bit like the first time you held a baby: Your initial instinct will be to kind of awkwardly grab it by the neck and poke it with your fingers until it emits a terrible shrieking sound. But if you break a guitar, it's not like a girl can just pop out a replacement from her vagina. Guitars must be held securely and treated with respect, not carelessly dragged around by their necks.

15

Guitar

Step 1:

Find a firm chair or couch. Once you're comfortably situated, rest the body of the guitar on your right leg, with its back against your chest.

Step 2:

Place the thumb of your left hand behind the neck of the guitar with your fingers poised above the strings. The neck should run parallel to the floor. Stay relaxed but try not to slouch. Bad posture makes playing more difficult and conveys a lack of confidence.

Guitar

Step 3:

You're ready to strum. Hold your right thumb and pointer fingers together as if making an "OK" sign. Now verify that the guitar is actually capable of producing sounds by strumming the tips of your fingers across the strings.

Your Guitar's Handedness

Your guitar should be right- or left-handed, consistent with your own handedness. To verify your guitar's handedness, make sure that as you hold the guitar, the topmost string is the thickest. To verify your own handedness, punch somebody in the back of the head and pay special attention to which hand you use.

On a left-handed guitar, the neck will extend to the right instead of the left. This means that southpaws must reverse some of the directions we provide in this chapter.

17

Almost Enough — Playing Chords

Before diving into the songs, let's quickly talk about chords. A chord is simply a collection of tones played simultaneously. There're hundreds of possible chord variations for the standard six-string guitar, and a great deal of them must be learned if you wish to be taken seriously as a musician. For those of us who simply wish to get laid, however, knowing so many chords would be like swatting a mosquito with an atomic bomb—reckless overkill.

The reality is that girls aren't counting how many chords you play. Without guidance, you can get by with a mere five. These five chords are: Em (E minor), C, A, G, and D.

Each of these chords is easy to play, and playing them in certain arrangements will produce recognizable songs women find irresistible. You will be like the fabled Pied Piper, hypnotizing women using the powers of your magic instrument. Except instead of leading children to their grisly deaths, you'll be leading women to a night of mediocre consensual sex.

 Blue Balls Beware

To reduce the risk that your music gives girls bleeding ears, splitting headaches, and vaginal dryness, you'll want to keep your guitar properly tuned. Thankfully, this isn't a problem, even if you're as tone deaf as we are. If you don't have access to an electric tuner, try typing "guitar tuner" into the search menu of your smartphone's app store.

Guitar

Your Instrument and You

Think of this as a picture of your guitar sitting in front of you. The six horizontal lines represent the six strings on your guitar (the top string being the thickest). The vertical lines represent **frets**, which are those metal bars used to separate notes.

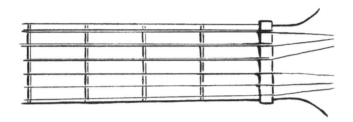

Placing Your Fingers on Your Instrument

Note the dots on the fingers in our illustrations. These dots represent which fingers should be clasping your guitar strings. Only clasp strings using the fingers indicated—your other fingers should not be in contact with the guitar.

Unless otherwise noted, your strumming hand should strum across all six strings.

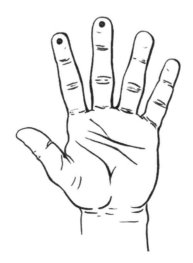

Just the Tip

Long fingernails will do nothing but hinder your strumming and your chord changes, The only one who is allowed to have long nails is her.

Step 1: Em (E Minor) chord

The Em (or E Minor) chord is a good place to start. Here's what it looks like:

Note that the finger positioning for the Em chord resembles the "sign of the horns" gesture commonly seen at rock concerts and especially good violin recitals.

The chord is played with your ring and middle finger in the second fret. These fingers should be placed firmly on each string to produce the truest notes. Also take care to avoid the fret bars themselves, or else you'll produce a muddled sound.

With your fingers properly situated, strum across all six strings with your right hand. Do this a few times, adjusting your fret hand fingers as necessary, until you hear crisp, clear notes. The resulting sound should be dark and brooding—which is perfect because that's how you come off when you play the guitar.

If this is your first time, you might find the experience to be painful and physically exhausting. Your inexperienced fingers will be sensitive as you contort them in ways you never previously imagined. Try to ignore the pain. As you build up calluses and develop rarely used muscles, each successive effort will be slightly less agonizing. But it might be a long road before you derive any actual pleasure from the process. Now you know how she feels.

VideoMark:
E Minor Chord

Just the Tip

Skip the pick. For our purposes, getting a guitar pick isn't necessary—and that makes it counterproductive. Your fingers have tips for a reason, and that reason is to play the acoustic guitar.

Step 2: D chord

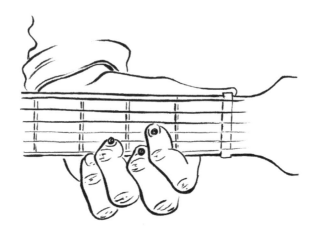

The trick to making the D chord easier to play is to position your ring finger where we've marked it in the third fret. In doing so, take care to avoid the bottom string or else you'll dull the sound of the chord. Your middle and pointer fingers will be easier to position in the second fret.

You might find that the D chord sounds a little better if you avoid the top two strings while strumming. If you find that impossible, don't lose any sleep over it. There are far better ways to lose sleep.

Just the Tip

If you're hearing an annoying "buzzing" sound as you play, or the sound of your strumming is interchangeable with that of a goat gnawing on the guitar, the likely culprit is that you're either not gripping your strings hard enough, or one of your fingers is touching a string or fret it shouldn't be. For the best results, keep your fingers toward the right side of the fret.

Step 3: A chord

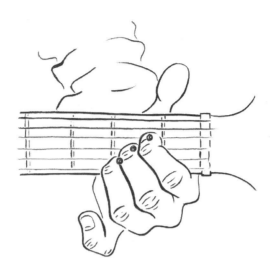

The A chord requires a bit more flexibility.

Your goal here is to cram three primary fingers all within the space of the second fret. To make enough room, your fingers should be placed adjacently—as opposed to directly on top of one another—so that they form a diagonal line. Naturally, you've also got to be careful to avoid touching the metal fret bars.

Since you lack a guitar player's dexterity, this may prove a bit challenging to coordinate, especially if you have fat fingers. It's somewhat acceptable to play the A chord using a lone middle or pointer finger against all three strings at once. If you try this approach, take care to arch your finger above the first string. The only real disadvantage here is that if your audience actually knows how to play the guitar, you will look a bit amateurish. In this case you may want to start angling for a sympathy lay.

Step 4: G chord

The G should be no problem for you. If there were somehow a song that relied exclusively on the G chord, this entire chapter would take 30 seconds. Unfortunately, doing nothing but repeatedly strumming the G chord is considered "irritating" and "an affront to the idea of music," if reactions to our "G Chord Rhapsody" demo tape are accurate.

Step 5: C chord

This will be the hardest chord you learn, but even this isn't too tall an order.

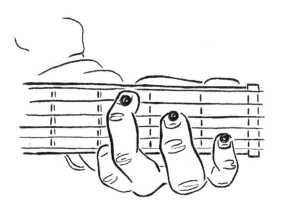

This finger arrangement might feel a bit awkward at first. If you've never played the guitar before, it's unlikely you've ever splayed your fingers quite like this.

If you aren't producing clean sounds right away, try playing each string individually until you find the off-sounding culprit, and then adjust that finger accordingly. Remember that your fingers should avoid touching any of the metal frets or adjacent strings. Also, keep your fingers firmly pressed against their assigned strings in the center of the space between fret bars.

Once you've got the C chord down, half of your work is over. Believe it or not, you now know the only five chords you'll ever need. At this point it's just a matter of playing them in the right order.

 View from a Broad

"Guys who play guitar are hot, sensitive, wild, artistic and crazy all at once. It's great."

Amy B., New York, NY

Step 6: A Little Back and Forth

Now that you feel somewhat comfortable playing each chord, let's work on the transitions between them. This will be the single most difficult part of this chapter, and unfortunately there's no getting around the necessity of a little repetition—but just a little. If practice makes perfect, a tiny bit of practice makes halfway decent, and that's probably good enough.

Transition 1: First try transitioning between the A and G a few times. You don't need to break any records for speed—just get used to moving your fingers back and forth between the chords.

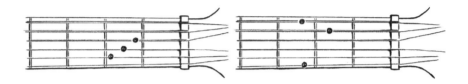

Transition 2: Now try C to G. Allow your fingers to get familiar enough with the transition so that both chords sound clean.

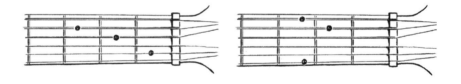

Just the Tip

You will get blisters on your fingertips. That's okay. Blisters are painful but eventually they'll lead to the formation of calluses. And calluses will lead to the formation of groupies. If you cry about your blisters, it'll be obvious you just started playing the guitar. And you'll probably just end up playing with yourself.

Guitar

Step 7: A Little Up and Down

Strumming is a common stumbling block for the begin-
ning guitarist. When should you strum up? When should
you strum down? Why are there so many choices? It can
begin to feel like you're trying to pull off a special move in
Mortal Kombat. You're just trying to play a song, not shoot
a fucking fireball.

Once you've gotten the hang of strumming, it's actually
the easiest part about playing the guitar. It becomes an
unconscious process pretty quickly. Strumming patterns
can change depending on the song, but it's always very
basic. It doesn't even matter how arrhythmic you are. If
you have the coordination to walk, you have the coordination to strum.

Just the Tip

When playing your guitar, make sure to strum
over the guitar's sound hole, which is that large
opening designed to project sound. Normally
we'd follow this advice up with an obvious lewd
reference based on the words "hole" and "large
opening," but the joke is too obvious, even for us.

The arrows below illustrate which direction to strum.
First try alternating between strumming up and down
with the A chord. Ideally, you'll want to be strumming at
regular intervals.

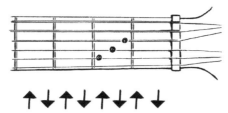

In the next example, notice that you do not strum on the third beat. When you get there, continue to move your arm as if you were still strumming, but don't actually play. This will help you keep time. Try to repeat this pattern:

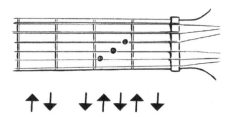

Now let's bring in what you learned from transitioning and combine it with strumming. Remember to avoid pausing between chords. As indicated, repeat this transition once going from A to Em.

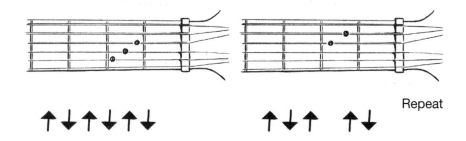

Repeat

VideoMark:
Strumming from A to Em

You should ultimately be capable of transitioning and strumming between any of the five chords. None of these sequences is more than you're capable of. Play around with them a bit and trust us—you'll find yourself improving rapidly. As you begin playing and strumming some of these chords in succession, you may start to notice odd, pleasant-sounding patterns. This is called music.

Just the Tip

If you are having trouble with any aspect of chord transitions or strumming, slow it down a notch. You're not in a death metal band. It's better to be slow and precise than fast and sloppy. At least that's what she said.

Just Enough — Playing Songs

You've spent countless minutes learning some basic chords and transitions. Now it's time for all of your halfhearted efforts to pay off.

These songs share similar DNA: They're easy to play and highly recognizable, and they provoke a Pavlovian vocal response in girls: "Oh, I *love* this song!" You may not be equipped to play any song she requests, but after playing her these crowd-pleasing tunes, the only thing she's likely to request is that you wear protection.

Jane's Addiction

"Jane Says"

Jane's Addiction guitarist Dave Navarro hardly needed to become a musician to get girls. Just look at the man's jaw line. There are perfectly straight men who would happily sleep with Dave Navarro. It's safe to say that vocalist Perry Farrell, however, probably benefited from being an alt-rock icon. Without inescapably catchy hits like "Jane Says," he's a squirrely eccentric with the shape and approximate weight of a kitchen broom. With his music? It wouldn't shock us if he's had more models than *The Price Is Right*.

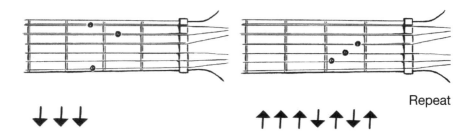

Repeat

VideoMark:
Playing "Jane Says"

Van Morrison

"Brown Eyed Girl"

Morrison was casting a pretty wide net when he wrote this classic-rock staple. More than half of the world's population has brown eyes, so for any given girl there's a better-than-50/50 chance this song has personal significance. She'll think this song is about her, and that'll make her feel special—even though brown eyes are by definition the least special eye color. Morrison might as well have written a song called "Right-Handed Girl" or "Girl Who Is Not Currently in a Coma." Or maybe something that would have applied to every female: "Girl Who Is into Dudes Who Can Play the Guitar."

Part 1

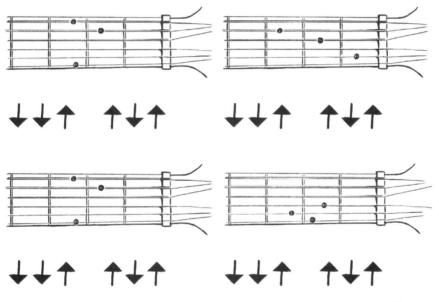

Repeat Part 1

VideoMark:
Playing Part 1 of
"Brown Eyed Girl"

Part 2

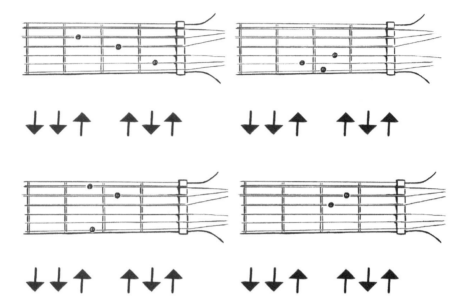

↓↓↑ ↑↓↑   ↓↓↑ ↑↓↑

↓↓↑ ↑↓↑   ↓↓↑ ↑↓↑

Repeat Part 2

VideoMark:
Playing Part 2 of
"Brown Eyed Girl"

Blue Balls Beware

If you doubt your vocal abilities, do not attempt
to sing. Have her sing the words, or just let your
guitar do the singing. Your atonal warbling will
detract attention from your guitar playing, and
that would defeat the entire purpose of this
chapter. Don't risk letting all those countless
minutes of practice go to waste.

Pearl Jam

"Last Kiss"

When Eddie Vedder wrote "Last Kiss" he really had your "first time" in mind. Yes, this melodic masterpiece is about a man who loses the love of his life in a car crash due to his bad driving. But it's deeper meaning is about reuniting with his "true love" in heaven. And who the hell can resist a song about true love. Not any girl we know. So by all means, use these chords to get yourself laid. The girl who was in the car accident would've wanted it that way.

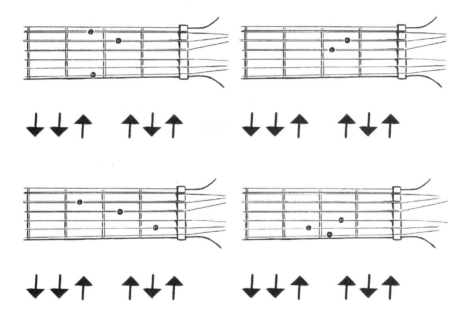

VideoMark:
Playing "Last Kiss"

A Sure Thing —Writing Your Own Music

The exact moment a girl concedes to your sexual advances is impossible to forecast. For some girls, merely alluding to the idea of a guitar will be enough; for others, playing a full chorus to one of the songs we've provided will do the trick. In any case, the un-predictable criterion for the vast majority of women will have been satisfied from the information we've already covered.

However, there is an upper echelon of desirables who won't be impressed. In all likelihood, they will have already seen suitors making these sorts of guitar-based advances. It is further plau-sible that these gentlemen had far greater skill than you. This will complicate your efforts by setting unreasonably high standards of proficiency. We've been anticipating these bastards, and you can impress this girl yet. The most reliable method for musically swooning your way into her heart-patterned panties is letting her be the first to hear the "new song" you yourself are working on.

In the spirit of learning just enough, we've designed a simple, customizable solution for composing a misleadingly soulful mas-terpiece in minutes. Even if you come from a loving, well-rounded family where punishments were only doled out in the form of hugs, we will show you how to assemble a tortured "I've been through it all" opus that'll have her comforting you through the night.

Title Your Masterpiece

A good title will set the mood for your song. To maximize the swooning potential, make it something mysterious. Avoid clichés. Be creative. Or if you're going to plagiarize, at least do it in a creative way.

Take a gander at the opinion section of any major news-paper. Editors regularly come up with short, intriguing headlines for letters to the editor and op-ed columns, and some of these make great song titles. Here are a few gems we found in one quick search: "Why I'm Leaving," "Still Needed," "Goodbye to All That." Or the simple one-word title that says very little but could have numerous meanings: "Don't."

Write the Music

Composing music is not as difficult as it sounds. The five chords we've taught you sound great in almost any sequence. If you manage to make an unpleasant song with these chords, you have a special talent for writing bad music and should be producing for Creed.

You can begin writing your own music just by starting to transition between chords you haven't played together yet. Keep your ears open for pleasant combinations. When you've found something you like, mold it into a simple pattern.

Your result may not be the most earth-shattering song in the world, but with the filter of a few beers, it may sound like a promising work-in-progress. At the very least, it definitely won't sound like you wrote it in 15 minutes. Which you didn't. You took no longer than 10.

How a Song Is Constructed

If the last significant thing you wrote was a drunken text message to your ex-girlfriend, writing a song may sound like a great deal of work. But the process is not difficult if you break it down into its fundamental parts. All you really need to worry about is coming up with a verse and figuring out a chorus.

A **verse** is a stanza of music. Each of your verses will have an identical chord structure but with alternate lyrics.

A **chorus** is the catchy melodic part of your song— a chance to really belt out your emotions. Lyrically, it's the thematic climax of your verses and will often contain the song's title. Each repetition of the chorus will be played identically with both the same lyrics and the same chord pattern.

In playing around with chords, a good rule of thumb is that if a pattern you like is subtler and more rhythmic, use it as your verse. If the pattern sounds like it could make a memorable hook, make it your chorus. If you find two patterns that sound nice in succession, you've got your song. All you really need are these two complementary patterns.

A song can be structured as simply as verse/chorus/ verse/chorus. Once you've got your two chord structures figured out, plug in some creative lyrics. And that's it.

Congratulations are in order. Just yesterday you were what can only be described as mentally guitarded. Now you can play five distinct chords in any order, and perhaps you've even written a song or two. We encourage you to keep learning the instrument, but as it is, you've already learned more than enough to attract girls. And you can rest assured that you can now play more chords than any member of Nickleback.

Wine

Not Quite Enough — Blowing Your Cork

Almost Enough — Storing, Serving, Pouring

Just Enough — Winocology

A Sure Thing — Wine Tasting

*W*ine has been around for as long as we've had an organized society. This is probably due to the fact that wine makes organized society tolerable. It is the drink of gods, the sanctifier of marriages, the best way to endure a family gathering—and the only truly respectable path to shattering your date's inhibitions. Whereas beer is commonly associated with the lowbrow, and hard liquor too clumsily reveals your intentions, wine delivers a smooth intoxication masked by a veneer of sophistication. It is, as Scottish novelist Robert Louis Stevenson once wrote, "bottled poetry." Which is to say that it's the world's most refined way to get drunk.

A standard-size wine bottle contains 750 milliliters, which is French for about four and a half glasses. If you're bad at math, this means that sharing a bottle will give her just enough of a buzz to start thinking you're attractive—and give you just enough of a buzz to fabricate plausible-sounding life aspirations. Wine is also a topic of conversation in and of itself; each bottle is intended to be discussed and pontificated upon, its merits weighed, its ultimate value appraised. You will find yourself sayings things like: "Hmm! The playful cedarwood notes really give this wine depth. And you can really taste the distinct undertones of buttercream almond chutney." As you become more comfortable, try describing flavors that don't actually even exist. "This Pinot Noir is exquisite. I think I'm tasting hints of unicorn tears."

All of this is, of course, probably horseshit. Your palate likely couldn't distinguish between a rich, earthy Pinot Noir and bathtub gin mixed with grape juice. Studies have indicated that even professional tasters sometimes have trouble distinguishing between midrange and top-shelf wines when given blind taste tests. The takeaway of this is that tasting wine can be thought of as a personal experience, open to interpretation. In other words, it's a great pastime for anybody with a proclivity for bullshitting (like people with liberal arts degrees).

Wine-tasting is also a can't-miss opportunity to garner some instant style points. Unless you're buying it in an unlabeled jug or a container made of cardboard, wine reeks of class. People do not chug wine or play wine pong, they do not take body shots of wine, and they rarely, if ever, pour out glasses of wine in honor of their fallen homies. And the pedestal on which wine is placed is not arbitrary. Wine has earned its position because of its rich history, the artistry of its creation and the complexity of the final product, which is designed to engage your sense of taste with the same intensity a boxing match engages your sense of touch.

Then again, what's going to help you on your next date is not wine's cultural significance, but the here and now of wine: knowing its various classifications, pairing it with your meal, properly pouring and tasting it, and being capable of bullshitting about it afterward.

For all the affected language that comes with discussing wine, it does provide some genuine sensual depths worth taking the time to explore. And if those complexities succeed in helping you get laid, it wouldn't be the first time wine has been associated with miracles.

The Bare Necessities

Several bottles of wine, corkscrew, wine glasses, foil cutter (optional), enough wine-tasting terminology to fake an advanced palate, high tolerances for both alcohol and pretentious banter.

Not Quite Enough — Blowing Your Cork

Struggling to open a bottle of wine is every bit as bad a mood killer as fumbling with a condom. And breaking either can lead to unspeakable disaster. You won't get anyone pregnant with a broken cork, but you do stand to ruin a perfectly good Shiraz, which could be far worse (depending on the vintage).

Just the Tip

Some makers of fine wine have switched to screw caps or synthetic corks. We recommend you avoid buying wine that takes one of these approaches. Although they're ultimately a more effective way to safeguard wine, they still have the stigma of cheapness and irreverence. Your priority should be to play it safe and side with tradition. If your date sees you unscrewing a cap and is unfamiliar with contemporary wine culture, she's liable to assume the Dollar Tree got itself a liquor license.

Removing the Foil

The first step to opening a bottle of wine is to remove the foil covering the cork. Many corkscrews include a built-in cutting tool expressly for this purpose. The key is to cut away from your hand, so that no matter how wild your follow-through, you'll be slashing air instead of your skin.

If you want to make it seem like you treat wine drinking as seriously as Batman treats crime fighting, you might want to invest in a stand-alone foil cutter. This little gadget is a nifty wishbone-shaped invention with two small, hidden blades like a cigar cutter. A simple squeeze and twist of its two halves will remove a perfect circle of foil every time.

Types of Corkscrews

Which corkscrew you decide to purchase (or find lying around your drawer) says a lot about your personality. Or it says a lot about what variety of corkscrew your local grocery store decided to stock. Either way, whichever style of screw you choose, uncorking a bottle of wine correctly should take no more effort than opening a bottle of beer—and should be significantly easier than opening up those infernal Capri Sun pouches.

Sommelier Knife

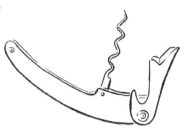

The sommelier knife is the ubiquitous, compact, Swiss Army knife-style corkscrew that appeals to minimalist sensibilities. A small knife unfolds from the sommelier knife's housing to deal with the foil. This is an extremely popular little corkscrew, and it's always impressive to get the job done with a smaller tool.

VideoMark:
Sommelier Knife

1. Once you've dispatched with the foil, close the knife and unfold the corkscrew. While holding the bottle's neck with your nondominant hand, place the tip of the cork-screw at the center of the cork. Note that the corkscrew ends at a 45-degree angle. Don't insert your corkscrew straight down—follow the angle of the corkscrew so that the tip is entered at a slant.

2. You may have promised the cork you'd just be entering your tip, but that was only a ploy—it's necessary to penetrate deeper. After you've inserted the tip, straighten the corkscrew. Applying steady downward pressure, gradually twist the corkscrew clockwise into the center of the cork until it's almost all the way in.

3. Unfold the hinge and brace it against the lip of the bottle.

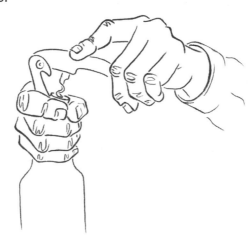

4. Lift the handle straight up to begin pulling out the cork. This shouldn't be too hard, as you're probably quite familiar with the pull-out method.

5. After lifting up the handle all the way, you may still need to jostle out the cork the rest of the way. Take your time with this at first, or else you'll risk snapping the cork—and your odds of getting laid—in half.

66,9
Quintessential Quotation

"Appreciating old wine is like making love to a very old lady. It is possible. It can even be enjoyable. But it requires a bit of imagination."

—Andre Tchelistcheff

The Wing Corkscrew

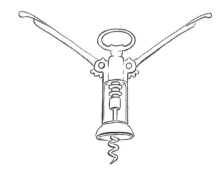

Another popular style of screw is the wing corkscrew, also called the butterfly or angel corkscrew. Its symmetrical, utilitarian design makes uncorking a bottle of wine simple enough to do in your sleep—although, if you're literally uncorking bottles of wine in your sleep, you should probably check yourself into a 12-step program. Everyone else should check themselves into the following (much easier to follow) three-step program:

1. After removing the foil, use your nondominant hand to grab the neck of the bottle and the corkscrew beneath its "wings." Direct the tip of the screw into the center of the cork.

2. With your other hand, twist the opener at its head. The wings will rise in tandem as the screw drives into the cork.

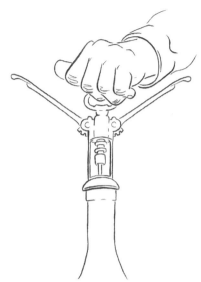

3. When they're in the reach-for-the-sky position, squeeze the wings back together to pop the cork. And that's it. If only it were that easy to take your date's top off.

VideoMark:
The Wing Corkscrew

Wine

Almost Enough — Storing, Serving, Pouring

Wine is like a demanding bride. Everything must be perfect—the lighting, the temperature, the ambience—or it will metamorphose into a terrifying, unrecognizable state. Achieving perfection means properly storing the wine, chilling it to the best serving temperature, drinking it from the right glass and pouring it with panache. This might be three or four steps beyond your usual libation-enjoying routine of bonging warm beer through an unwashed funnel, but your diligence will pay dividends. An inexpensive wine served properly is more satisfying than a top-shelf wine consumed at room temperature in your limited-edition Iron Man thermos.

Storing

Heat is the mortal enemy of wine. So your top priority in storing wine is preventing prolonged exposure to heat, which can turn wine into vinegar. This would be nice on a salad but tends to go over poorly by the glass.

You might be tempted to combat the problem with refrigerator storage. While this is okay for a couple of days, the frequent variation in fridge temperature (caused by opening and closing the door during commercial breaks, prescription-drug-induced sleep-eating, trying to figure out if the light stays on, etc.) shrinks and expands the wine's cork, breaking its seal with the bottle and allowing air to corrupt your wine's delicate constitution.

Light is also an asshole to wine. The UV rays in sunlight and fluorescent lighting do no favors to its flavor. Humidity, meanwhile, is dangerous in either extreme. Too much humidity can cause mold to grow, while too little can cause cork shrinkage—an outcome with which we're all too familiar.

Ideal Storage

Since you're probably not looking to shell out a couple hundred bucks on a custom-built temperature- and humidity-controlled wine cellar, your next best option is a cool, dark closet. Storing your bottles on their sides, either in a wine rack or on the floor, keeps the corks in contact with the wine and thus moist, preventing your cork from shriveling up like Grandma's prunes.

Buzzkill

Heat, prolonged refrigeration, light and extreme levels of humidity.

Serving

Serving wine is a bit like foreplay. You wouldn't just grab your date by the neck, spin her upside down and start pounding away. Imbibing a 2007 Chardonnay isn't any different. Taking your time on the details before you get to the drinking will make the indulgence that much more rewarding for both of you.

Serving Temperature

Many people believe that red wines should be served at room temperature, but this is a misconception. Reds have a thermal sweet spot, and it's generally not where you've set your thermostat.

White wine—60 minutes of refrigeration.
Red wine—20 to 30 minutes of refrigeration.

We're not the first to say it, but the vessel from which you drink is as fundamental to the drinking experience as the liquid itself. Drink from the Holy Grail and you'll be endowed with immortality; drink from a homeless man's shoe and the only thing you'll be endowed with is gonorrhea.

Serving Glasses

Stemware

Stemware features a round base connected to a rounded bowl by a thin stem, which is designed to prevent your hands from transmitting heat to the wine. There are distinct sizes and shapes of stemware corresponding to virtually every variation of wine, but for the most part these stylistic conventions can be disregarded. As long as you've got a few traditional red and white wine glasses in your cupboard, you're in good shape.

White Wine Glass

The diverging shapes of white and red wine glasses are not merely a ploy to trick us into buying more glasses than we justifiably need. White wine glasses are narrower for two reasons: Aeration is not as important as it is in reds, and the slimmer bowl allows the wine to stay cooler longer.

Red Wine Glass

The large bowl of a red wine glass facilitates the chemical interaction of wine with oxygen, which brings out its full flavor and aroma. It's also designed to be swirled, which further helps this process of aeration, and further helps maximize the snobby, high-society bearing of an experienced wine drinker.

Tumblers

Hip, cutting-edge restaurants are increasingly serving wine in folksy tumblers, and if you're feeling a bit daring you can follow suit. This can be less tradition-busting than wallet-protecting, as tumblers are harder to break. (This is especially convenient when you're drunk.)

Buzzkill

Solo cups, anything with NASCAR written on it, Starbucks mugs, baby bottles.

Pouring Wine

You'll want your pour to be slightly less than half-full. A full wine glass will come off as a transparent attempt to tranquilize your date into a state of inebriated compliance. You're trying to enjoy a bottle of wine with a girl, not drug her. Moreover, wine heats up in a room-temperature glass much faster than in a properly chilled bottle, so over-pouring will make the last few mouthfuls unpleasantly warm, as though you were downing wounded soldiers at the tail end of a house party, and not having a romantic night at home with a sophisticated girl and a plucky, overachieving Pinot.

Buzzkill

Pouring your own glass first, sloppy spilling, drinking directly from the bottle.

Ideal Pour

To prevent messes, wrap a clean dishtowel or napkin around the neck of your bottle. It also helps to twist the bottle slightly as you finish pouring to slow the forward momentum of those last few drops and encourage them back into the bottle.

View from a Broad

"A guy who knows a lot about wine seems worldly, even if he's never left his home state. Like he has all kinds of things to teach me."

Carrie, Providence, RI

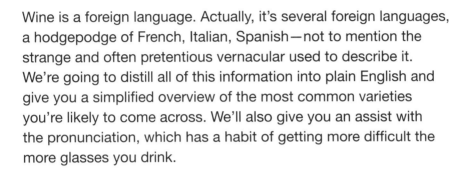

Just Enough —Winocology

Wine is a foreign language. Actually, it's several foreign languages, a hodgepodge of French, Italian, Spanish—not to mention the strange and often pretentious vernacular used to describe it. We're going to distill all of this information into plain English and give you a simplified overview of the most common varieties you're likely to come across. We'll also give you an assist with the pronunciation, which has a habit of getting more difficult the more glasses you drink.

Of course, it's not just about finding the right wine. It's also about describing the characteristics of that wine in such a way that you seem like an authority on the subject, even if the only thing you really know about wine is how much you can drink before blacking out.

You probably never sat around the lunch table describing your glass of Kool-Aid as "biscuity," "peppery" or "oily." This is because they made it easy on us by printing the flavor on the bag; and if you still couldn't figure it out, that big-ass Kool-Aid pitcher would probably burst through the wall and shout the flavor at your face. This lack of subtlety is not embraced at the winery, where patrons are forced to determine a wine's flavor profile through sheer aimless speculation. Describing wine is therefore afforded a certain degree of poetic license. On the next page are a few particularly useful terms (and a couple others to avoid).

Buzzkill

Mispronouncing wines, sniffing corks, chewing gum while you drink wine, asking your waiter to bring you the restaurant's "finest box of wine."

On Good Terms

Body: This characteristic is often referred to as "mouthfeel" because it describes the way a wine feels in your mouth, especially in regard to the sense of alcohol.

Fruit: To say that a wine has "good fruit" or is "fruit forward" means that there is a pleasing sweetness to it. Wine that is overly sweet can be dismissed as "cloying."

Juiciness: To say that a wine is "juicy" means that it has a refreshing acidity. A wine's acidity is what makes our mouth water and stimulates our appetites. Wines described as "juicy" tend to be more food-friendly.

Tannins: When the red wine you're drinking gives you a mild case of cotton mouth, you're dealing with tannins. Tannins are a group of chemical compounds produced by the skins, stems and seeds of wine grapes. Though extremely tannic wines can result in unpleasantness (you could call it "austere" or "coarse"), when present in moderation they can yield a smooth, velvety mouthfeel.

Terroir (tare-wah): The French word for "land," terroir is a concept in winemaking and wine appreciation that relates to how the environment (location, soil, climate) in which the grapes are grown shapes the wine's flavor.

Terms to Avoid

Dry: Dry is probably the most overused word in the wine world. Since all it means is "not sweet," the only time it functions as a handy descriptor is when it's used to distinguish itself from wines that are normally thought of as being sweet—i.e., "a dry Riesling". To walk into a wine shop and say that you'd like a dry red wine is to say, "I am interested in every red wine in this shop except for those three bottles in the dessert section."

Varietal: The biggest faux pas currently being committed is describing different types of grapes as "varietals" instead of "varieties." A "varietal wine" is a term used to denote a wine that is made from a single grape variety, as opposed to blends.

White Wines

We're putting the whites in order from lightest-bodied to heaviest-bodied. Wine, like beer (and women), comes in a wide range of bodies. Just as a lager is lighter than an amber ale, which is lighter than a stout or porter, a Pinot Grigio is lighter than a Sauvignon Blanc, which is lighter than a Chardonnay. It's not a question of color (though that often goes hand in hand)—it's a question of thickness, texture and intensity of flavor. Which wine is right for you depends upon your personal preferences, the food you're pairing it with and, most importantly, the type of girl you're looking to cork.

Anatomy Lesson

Food-Pairing Key

Cheese   Cheese and   Dessert   Fish
Crackers

Fried Food   Hamburger   Hot Dog   Lamb

Pizza   Poultry   Pork   Red Meat

Salad   Shellfish   Spicy Food   Stew

Strawberry   Sushi

Pinot Gris (PEE-no-GREES) Pinot Grigio (PEE-no-GREE-jo):

> **Girl Pairing:** This wine tends to be a favorite among risk-averse, shallow-end-of-the-pool girls not looking to put anything unfamiliar in their mouths. If it were a sexual position, it would be missionary position, bra on and lights out.
>
> **Associated Terms:** Light, crisp, easy-drinkin'
>
> **Food Pairing:**

It's the wine equivalent of an ice-cold beer on a hot summer day. Though grown all over the world and running the gamut from clean and crisp to rich and floral, Pinot Grigio—or Pinot Gris depending on where it's from—is probably most remarkable for its unremarkability. This isn't necessarily a bad thing—even the biggest oenophiles occasionally want to drink something they don't have to think too hard about. You may find yourself tasting pears and lemon with a hint of flowers thrown in, but you won't exactly be overwhelmed by the complexity. Like a sorority girl, it's light, simple, and goes down easy.

Sauvignon Blanc (soh-vin-yohn blahngk):

> **Girl Pairing:** This girl has a little edge to her—not quite a "labia-piercing" edge, but she's definitely been around the Sauvignon block.
>
> **Associated Terms:** tart, herbal, minerally, citrusy
>
> **Food Pairing:**

Sauvignon Blancs rival Pinot Grigios in terms of drinkability, and they also possess a distinctive crispness that makes them more refreshing and often a lot more interesting. There's a lot of naturally occurring acid in the grape, which gives it a tartness you'd find in tangier citrus fruits like limes and grapefruit. This is balanced by an herbal or grassy quality. If you've ever had a shot of wheatgrass at a health food store or farmers' market, you'll know the kind of flavor we're talking about. With all these flavors in the same glass, Sauvignon Blanc is an easy wine to pair with food. It's like a plaid shirt: whatever color pants you grab, it probably works.

 On Good Terms

Old World Wine: Refers to the classic wine-making regions in Europe and emphasizes tradition and the importance of a wine's terroir. It is associated with *place*.

New World Wine: Refers to wine made any-where outside of Europe, including South America, the United States, Australia, and Mexico. New World Wine emphasizes the scientific aspects of winemaking and has a reputation for being fruitier, more oaky, and more alcoholic. It is associated with *process*.

Riesling (reez-ling):

Girl Pairing: She seems sweet on the surface, but one day you'll wake up and find your apartment ransacked and a fork jammed in your neck.

Associated Terms: tangy, aromatic, versatile

Food Pairing:

Perhaps no wine is in greater need of a good PR campaign than Riesling. In the minds of most Americans, Riesling is just a shade drier than high-fructose corn syrup, and enjoyed only by little old ladies and diabetics in training. The truth is that Riesling (primarily produced in German, Austria and France) is one of the world's most versatile grape varieties, producing wines that vary from bone-dry to syrupy sweet.

And the irony is that it was America's collective sweet tooth that compelled importers to seek out only the most freakishly sweet Rieslings from the Old World and produce similarly sugary ones in the New World. The best, off-dry (i.e., slightly sweet) Rieslings are bold, balanced and super-food-friendly, often contrasting fruit-forward notes of peaches, apples or melon with a juicy acidity and/or a crisp minerality.

Chardonnay (shard-uh-nay):

Girl Pairing:
Old World: She wears the pantsuit in the relationship.
New World: She only wears underwear on special occasions.

Associated Terms:
Old World: Tense, acidic, crisp
New World: Buttery, oaky, rich

Food Pairing:
Old World:

New World:

Chardonnay is the Dr. Jekyll and Mr. Hyde of wine. Most Old World examples run a pretty narrow range from crisp and easy-drinking to tense, tart and acidic—like biting into a barely ripe green apple. However, over the last few decades, the trend on this side of the pond has been to take these rather nondescript grapes and, through various tricks of the trade, turn them into full-bodied, highly oaked (whether from barrel aging or the addition of wood chips), high-alcohol behemoths.

Like dog breeders who selectively distort the natural proportions of pugs until they can barely breathe, these wineries put their wine in ever-newer barrels (which impart more flavor than older barrels) for ever-longer periods of time, until drinking a California Chardonnay can be like sucking butter through a wooden straw. These wines are called "oak bombs," and that might not even go far enough. Some of them should literally be banned from airports.

Red Wines

As we did with the white wines, we're going to list the reds in order from lightest- to heaviest-bodied. Red wines are considerably heartier and more complex than their lighter counterparts, which makes them particuarly rewarding for more advanced palates. Unfortunately, they can also give your teeth a not-so-subtle hue of disgusting. If you're on a first date, bring a toothbrush.

Pinot Noir (pee-noh nwahr):

Girl Pairing: She's a food-conscious environmentalist who shops at Walmart; an animal-lover who scalps tickets to dog fights.

Associated Terms: silky, earthy, versatile, light-medium-bodied

Food Pairing:

Pinot Noir from the United States tends to be slightly fuller, fruitier, higher in alcohol and less acidic than its forefathers in France's Burgundy region. Regardless of where they're from, the best Pinots share many of the same oxymoronic characteristics: They manage to be earthy yet fruity; light- to medium-bodied yet rich in flavor. A food-lover's wine, it goes with basically everything. You can think of it as the gateway drug to heavier red wines.

Merlot (mur-loh):

Girl Pairing: She's a plain Jane, no-surprises kind of girl. If she pulled up next to you at a stoplight, you could surmise everything about her in the time it takes the light to change.

Associated Terms: smooth, soft, fruity with common notes of plum and dark berries

Food Pairing:

Smooth as a baby's ass with notes of dark fruit and little to no tannin, Merlot is the wine of choice if you're clamoring for a soft, highly drinkable wine, but it has all the excitement of a preseason WNBA game. This makes it very accessible for neophytes, but seasoned wine snobs tend to regard it as unworthy of their precious palates and wouldn't put it in their mouths unless they were out of mouthwash.

Syrah or Shiraz (sir-ah, sure-oz):

Girl Pairing: She says what's on her mind and could possibly take you in a fight in a neutral setting.

Associated Terms: full-bodied, fruit-forward, peppery, spicy

Food Pairing:

Popular worldwide, Syrah's flavor profile varies a bit depending on where it's from. French Syrahs tend to be earthy with notes of raspberries, while their New World cousins are more fruit-forward, spicy and higher in alcohol. Syrah has become extremely popular in Australia, where it's branded as Shiraz and skews more jammy and full-bodied. In all cases, it's a drier, darker wine; it hits like a heavyweight (think George Foreman) and is great with grilling (again George Foreman).

Cabernet Sauvignon (cab-er-nay so-vin-yawn):

Girl Pairing: She's got a lot going on. She's well educated and multitalented, and although she makes 20 percent more than you, somehow you still have to pay for everything.

Associated Terms: rich, complex, hearty, tannic, earthy, herbal

Food Pairing:

Cabernet Sauvignon, the most popular and often most expensive of the reds, is a distinctive, full-bodied wine beloved for its complex, layered flavors. Most Cabernets mingle elements of dark fruit and mint with a pronounced earthiness (Cabs are renowned

for their ability to reflect their terroir). This is further complicated by notes of vanilla and smoke from time spent in oak barrels. To the uninitiated palate, or when drunk on its own without rich, fatty food to act as a foil, the complex power of Cabernet Sauvignon could prove a bit overwhelming. Don't unleash this Pandora's bottle unless you know your date is up to the task.

Zinfandel (zin-fin-dell):

Girl Pairing: Extroverted girls who drink heavily and wear those irritatingly large sunglasses.

Associated Terms: jammy, brambly (referring to bramble fruits like blackberries and raspberries), rich, robust

Food Pairing:

Zinfandel is often summed up in one word: jammy. You almost can't describe this rich, medium-to full-bodied wine without the word. You might taste raspberries, blackberries, blueberries, Crunch Berries—pretty much anything ending in "berry." And though some New World winemakers have gotten a bit mad scientist with their Zinfandels (producing heavily oaked, high-alcohol abominations of nature), many elegant examples are being produced in California that balance out all the jam with a little acidity and some soft tannins.

On Good Terms

The year on the bottle of the wine is called the "vintage." Since weather and other factors fluctuate each year, so does the quality of the grape.

Wines of a Different Color

Rosé (roh-zey):

Girl Pairing: She's vivacious and perky, to the extent that she wears pink dresses and flip-flops to funerals.

Associated Terms: light, crisp, fruity, juicy

Food Pairing:

We know. You're supposed to turn up your nose at Rosés because they're pink, but even the paragons of snobbery (Parisians) drink it while vacationing on the French Riviera. It's perfect on a hot, sunny day as an accompaniment to anything hauled out of the ocean. Full of flavor but light as air, it's the Pringles of wine.

Thanks to posers like "White Zinfandel" and "Blush," Rosé (much like Riesling) has suffered in the states from its reputation as a cloyingly sweet, grandma wine. Nothing could be further from the truth. Traditional dry rosés are light, crisp (sometimes minerally and complex) and groin-grabbingly refreshing, coming about as close to thirst-quenching as an alcoholic beverage can get. This is the definitive wine for picnics in the park and bonfires on the beach.

Sparkling Wines:

Girl Pairing: She doesn't go to parties, she hosts them— and then gets so drunk she demands somebody give her a ride home.

Associated Terms: effervescent, crisp, romantic, festive

Food Pairing:

The cardinal rule of sparkling wines is that you can't call them Champagne unless they're from Champagne (a province in northeastern France). How would you know if the bottle you're drinking is from Champagne? Aside from the fact that it will say so on the bottle, it will probably cost you a king's ransom. Unless you're so loaded that, like Biggie, you "sip champagne when [you're] thirstay," dropping half your paycheck on a bottle may be a little presumptuous for a first date.

Fortunately you can't patent bubbles, so there're plenty of amazing dry sparkling white wines from outside Champagne that you can find in the $10 to $20 range. French Cremants offer much of the same yeasty nose and complexity of flavor as Champagne but often at half the price, while Spanish Cavas and Italian Proseccos make a slightly leaner, fruitier, but ultimately dry and refreshing alternative.

A Sure Thing — Wine Tasting

Wine tastings are the perfect storm of dates: They're inexpensive, refined as shit, and can lead to a pretty good buzz before sunset. You don't need to live near Napa Valley to find a decent winery, either. They've sprung up all over the country, in every state. If there're somehow none within a convenient drive, however, your local wine shop probably offers up regular wine tastings. They're the perfect opportunity to appraise a subject you're not really equipped to evaluate while dispensing unholy truckloads of bullshit.

Examine the Hue

Being the observant person you are, the first thing you might notice at a wine tasting is the color of the wine. And just as Eskimos are famous for having dozens of words for snow and girls for having limitless ways to refer to the color of white walls (eggshell, ivory, pearl, off-white, on-white, reverse-white), wine is famous for the many ways there are to describe its color. Half the time it's pretty obvious people are just making these colors up. And who's going to stop them? You don't know the difference. Now it's your chance to get back at them.

Hold your glass up to the light to examine the color. If it's a white, don't just say it looks white—it already says that on the menu. Instead call it:

- Golden
- Goldenrod
- Straw
- Hay
- Amber
- Motor oil
- Pee-pee

If it's red, call it:

- Ruby
- Magenta
- Burgundy
- Scarlet
- Crimson
- Maroon
- Menstrual

You can even throw some fruits and veggies out there:

- Plum
- Raspberry
- Beet
- Rhubarb
- Strawberry Pop-Tart

Swirl

Swirling your glass isn't merely an idle demonstration of how pompous you are—it's meant to let in oxygen and release a wine's aromas. To swirl, it's best to keep the glass on the counter to reduce the risk of spillage. Deliver the effect with a masculine shoulder rotation while taking care not to send the liquid splashing over the rim of your glass onto your khakis.

Your wine should move in a pleasant whirlpool and climb up the sides of your glass. Once you stop swirling, the wine will stream down the glass unevenly, leaving streaks. In the wine community these are called legs, except by the overdramatic French, who call them tears. These will actually tell you nothing about the quality of the wine, just its alcohol content. Thick, slow-moving legs are indicative of more alcohol. If your date has thick, slow-moving legs, this can be quite helpful, as your game plan might require that both of you be sufficiently intoxicated.

Smelling the wine

Swirling also releases scents and aromas, and now it's time to take them in. Lean into the glass and breathe in deep. When describing the smell, let some of the associated terms we provided guide you. Is it a Zinfandel? You know what's coming: jammy. Is it a Chardonnay? Consider it oaky. Sauvignon Blanc? Smell that citrus.

Smell is mostly subjective, so again, you can pretty much blurt out the first thing you think of. Compare it to a food or plant; try describing the type of weather the smell evokes. Get creative, but don't stray into vulgarity. She probably won't be impressed if you say the wine smells like Strawberry Shortcake's vagina.

Here're some other smell-related words to consider:

- Peppery
- Buttery
- Clean
- Sulfury
- Yeasty
- Arousing
- Winealicious

Drinking

As fun as it can be to hover your nose over fermented grape juice while swirling your glass around like a fucking snow globe, none of this is going to be particularly satisfying, and it definitely won't get you drunk. So enough with the pretense—it's time to finally drink.

Actually, this isn't drinking the way you might be used to it, where the object is to actually ingest a meaningful quantity of liquid. You're still only supposed to sip at this point. You may remember from grade-school biology that different parts of the tongue pick up on different flavors. This is actually a grade-school misconception; all parts of your tongue can detect a multitude of tastes. Nevertheless, gently rolling the wine around your mouth will give more of your taste buds a chance to enjoy and evaluate it, and give you some time to formulate your reaction.

What did you taste? Feel free to use your newfound knowledge: "This Riesling is giving me peach notes." "I'm getting cinnamon

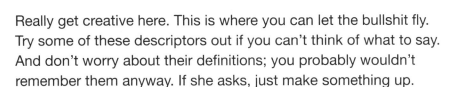

from this Cabernet." If it's red, the first berry that comes to mind will work. If it's white, you can't go wrong with pear or peach. Or throw something obscure out. It's not like she's going to call you out on it. "Elderberry? What the hell are you talking about, asshole? It's clearly more of a black truffle."

Really get creative here. This is where you can let the bullshit fly. Try some of these descriptors out if you can't think of what to say. And don't worry about their definitions; you probably wouldn't remember them anyway. If she asks, just make something up.

- Round
- Mellow
- Accessible
- Toasty
- Supple
- Jaunty
- Moist
- Nipply

After the wine's been swashed around the mouth a bit, some tasters prefer to spit, especially at a more formal tasting, because too much alcohol can affect the accuracy with which one evaluates wine. It's really one of the only times spitting is considered polite, along with watermelon-seed spitting contests and tractor pulls. Most casual wine tastings don't require spitting, of course—and you probably wouldn't mind the buzz—but the question of whether you spit or swallow is entirely up to you.

Once you've had your full allotment of tastings, discuss your favorites and pick up a bottle or two, because the festivities don't have to conclude at the winery. Uncork another bottle at your place and find out whether your date decides to spit or swallow in a somewhat more intimate context.

Cooking

Not Quite Enough — Before Putting Anything into Your Mouth

Almost Enough — Prep Talk

Just Enough — The Main Course

A Sure Thing — Just Desserts

*T*he average guy can't cook. Anything. Most of us could be locked in a kitchen stocked with unlimited ingredients, only to emerge piss-drunk two hours later, proudly showboating a piece of lettuce mysteriously wrapped around an undercooked potato and garnished with a half-eaten Pizza Pocket.

Our culinary inadequacies stem from a widespread (and dated) cultural misconception. Guys often dismiss the kitchen as an emasculating place designed for women to prepare and dispense sandwiches. We're afraid that getting flour on our hands will eventually lead to us cavorting around in a sundress and joining the local chapter of the Sisterhood of the Traveling Pants. More-over, when it comes to eating, males frequently find themselves taking the path of least resistance. We're lazy, and cooking seems like an overly involved optional step in between acquiring food and eating it.

Truth is, though, girls love a guy who knows his way around the stovetop, especially if he's capable of using one without giving the county fire marshal a heads up. Cooking food for a girl lights up the enigmatic part of her brain that she uses to decide whether or not she sleeps with you (we'll call it the full-frontal cortex). For one thing, having confidence in the kitchen demonstrates maturity. It shows that you're a provider and don't need to rely on your mommy (or Domino's) every time your stomach is empty, like some sort of fully grown baby. Girls don't want to feel that you need to be burped prior to intercourse, and tearfully consoled afterward.

And the best part about having a date in your own dining room is you've already got her back at your place. Consider this scenario: you're sitting across from your prospective bedmate at your dining room table. The two of you have just enjoyed a satisfying dish of Pan-Roasted Pork Loin Chops, and it was delicious in all respects, not to mention impressively presented.

Now the two of you are enjoying a reasonably priced Cabernet while she tells you which of her friends she thinks are complete bitches (hint: all of them). But what she's thinking is: "Wow, this guy is really willing to put effort into making me satisfied. I wonder if he's this attentive when the lights are out."

The skills laid before you will be well within your grasp even if you haven't been near a stove since that time you accidentally stumbled into the kitchen section of the Ikea showroom. We won't ask you to labor for more than 20 minutes in preparation, from cooking the meal to setting the table.

We're going to teach you several unassailable, palate-assaulting recipes—and although they'll look impressive, they don't take long to prepare and they cost much less than dinner for two at the Olive Garden. And after you and your partner have finished your appetizing, visually impressive home-cooked meal, trying to transition into the bedroom will be like attempting a maze with no dead ends. All roads lead to victory.

The Bare Necessities

- Skillet, 10″ or bigger
- Large stockpot
- Large chef's knife
- Medium-sized wooden spoon, although a small wooden spoon works just fine as long as you know what to do with it
- Spatula
- Tongs
- Whisk
- Colander
- Roasting pan or rimmed baking sheet
- Measuring cup
- Instant-read thermometer
- Presentable plates/glasses/silverware
- Offensively inaccurate Italian accent
- "Kiss Me, I'm a Cook!" underpants

On Good Terms

Boil: Cook by submerging in boiling water.

Braise: Slowly cook, using a combination of moist and dry heat. Often the food is first seared and then cooked with a liquid.

Grill: Cook using direct heat, either over open flames or on the stovetop using a grill pan.

Roast: Slowly cook using dry, indirect heat, usually in the oven.

Sauté: Quickly cook in a shallow pan on the stovetop, using direct heat and a little butter or oil.

Sear: Quickly cook the surface of a food so that a caramelized crust is formed.

Not Quite Enough — Before Putting Anything into Your Mouth

Before you even crack an egg, let's touch on some basic etiquette. The manner in which you serve and eat your food will go a long way in determining whether or not you'll have the opportunity to burn off some of that caloric energy in the bedroom afterward. It doesn't matter if these shortcuts to culinary competency help you discover a secret talent for braising your beef and you become the Food Network's next Iron Hard Chef—if you chew with your mouth open, the only juicy breasts in your future will come with a beak.

This is especially relevant to those of us who tend to eat our meals sprawled out on the couch using a napkin as our plate and our shirt as a napkin. If you're hosting another human being, all the little nuances of presentation and manners become as critical as the food itself. This is a short list—everything should be pretty obvious, so review it quickly, because practicing poor decorum at the dinner table is a surefire way to inadvertently save your virginity for marriage.

Don't talk with your mouth full: Talking too much can always ruin a date, but this is never truer than when you're in the process of chewing. Your dumb anecdote can wait until after you've swallowed. The last thing your date needs is food particles blasting out of your mouth like bullets from the spread gun in *Contra*, covering her in a patina of semidigested risotto. Your meal loses something in the presentation when it's served in this fashion.

Keep your elbows off the table: You've probably heard this from your mother ad nauseam, making this one of the few times you should think of dear ol' mom on a romantic date (along with when you're trying to last another five minutes longer). Keeping your arms off the table will prevent you from clumsily knocking over your own glass, but it's also important to consider when you're out with another couple. Your arms sprawled on all ends of the table is just as annoying to your neighbor as it was when your brother put his hand on "your" side of the car. The only personal space you should enter is your date's.

Put your fucking napkin on your lap: Almost as bad as eating with your mouth open is not hiding your slop rag. A napkin on your lap also frees up valuable table real estate and can save your pants from a nasty and difficult-to-explain chocolate stain. Keep in mind when cooking at home that a wad of Kleenex is not a viable substitute for napkins. Cloth napkins are best, but paper ones will do (as long as they don't say Taco Bell on the front).

You're not a caveman: When cutting food, place your index fingers on the tops of your utensils and don't cut more than one or two pieces of food off at a time. Your knife should be in your dominant hand.

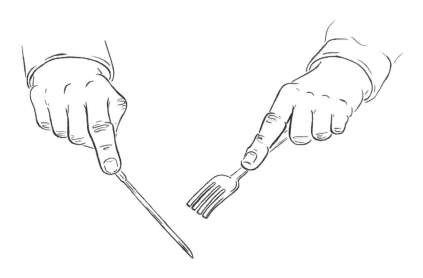

Once you're finished cutting, set down your knife and switch your fork back to your dominant hand. The fork should be resting loosely in between your middle finger and your thumb. Do not clench the fork with your entire fist as though you're trying to give it a happy ending.

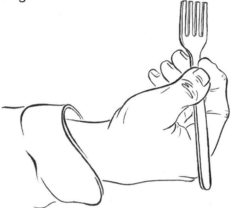

Place setting: While you don't want your dinner to have the rigid formality of a monocles-only banquet, there's something to be said for the quiet sophistication of a smartly arrayed table setting. Here's a standard arrangement:

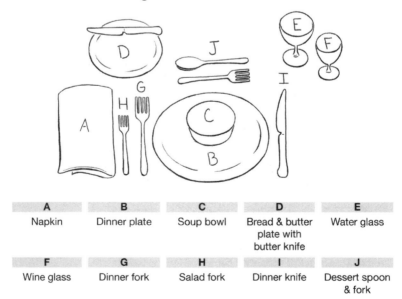

A	B	C	D	E
Napkin	Dinner plate	Soup bowl	Bread & butter plate with butter knife	Water glass

F	G	H	I	J
Wine glass	Dinner fork	Salad fork	Dinner knife	Dessert spoon & fork

Tablecloths: If you originally rescued your "dining" table from a dumpster and are embarrassed to use it for anything other than a hobo poker tournament, don't resort to firing up an illegal bonfire just yet; you might be able to conceal the problem. A tablecloth is significantly cheaper than a new piece of furniture and can transform a stained, parched, glorified beer pong table into a stained, parched, glorified beer pong table that is discreetly hidden beneath a sheet of clean cotton.

Tableware: If your plates and glasses are a chaotic mishmash of cracked crockery culled from garage sales or dead relatives, or it's been stolen from Bennigan's, it may be time to spring for a new set. Keep in mind that your dishware and silverware should look like they belong together, and both should appear clean. Plastic sporks and your Burger King *Dukes of Hazzard* mug are well coordinated, but this is not what we are talking about.

Almost Enough — Prep Talk

The kitchen can be a dangerous place. It's full of things that can stab you, asphyxiate you, and burn your flesh. So we're going to play this as safely as possible and defer to the teaching methods of our spiritual advisor, Mr. Miyagi. Just as young Daniel-san was forced to perform remedial and humiliating household chores before he was taught the awkward, off-balance, somehow-deadly crane kick, we too must embarrass you, young grasshopper. Geographic realities prevent us from tricking you into washing our cars and painting our houses, but we can still demean you with a handful of extremely simple kitchen lessons. Only then will you be prepared to attempt the Flaming Banana.

Boiling Water

Burner on, burner off. Burner on, burner off. Boiling water is about as simple a kitchen activity as you can find. But it's also potentially dangerous, and doing it incorrectly can ruin an entire dish. So bust out your tea bag and let's get to work.

Step 1:

Choose a pot large enough to contain both the food you're cooking and the water required to boil it. There should also be at least 3 inches of extra room on top so that the water doesn't boil over.

Step 2:

Set the burner to high, place the pot on the burner, and cover it with a lid.

Step 3:

Keep an eye on the water by lifting the lid every few minutes, preferably with a potholder to avoid scalding your hands. Contrary to the popular aphorism, watched pots do indeed boil. Moreover, unwatched pots can actually start kitchen fires.

Step 4:

Once the water is violently bubbling, your task is complete. You're now ready to move on to your next task. But don't think we've merely taught you how to boil water. The act of turning your burner's knob on and off has created the muscle memory required to properly arouse a nipple. Just kidding, that would probably hurt like hell. We mainly just taught you to boil water.

Just the Tip

Some cookbooks will tell you to add salt to make your water boil faster. Don't bother. The amount of salt added to a pot of boiling water won't make any meaningful difference. Save the salt for the wounds of your enemies.

The Facts of Knife

Watching someone clumsily hack into a tomato with the precision of a log splitter is like observing midgets playing full-court basketball: hilarious, but frustratingly futile. Basic knife skills are a must. Chunky tomato ketchup mush just doesn't offer the same allure as the same ingredient elegantly diced. Going forward you'll only need one versatile knife, so don't fall victim to door-to-door Cutco charlatans.

Blue Balls Beware

Resist the urge to try any Benihana-style grand-standing. What your date will find charming is your attempt to cook her dinner, not how many rotations you can flip your knife.

The Chef's Knife

How to hold your knife: Pinch the blade with your thumb and index finger to steady the blade. Wrap your other three fingers around the handle.

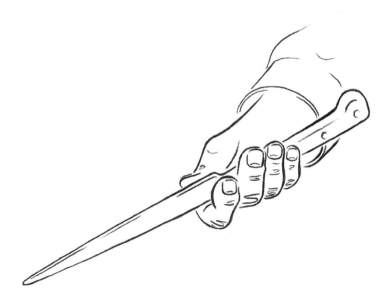

The knife should feel like an extension of your arm, like Edward Scissorhand's scissor hands.

How to hold the food: Blood, whether it's coming from you or her, is always a buzzkill on a date. Do your part by refraining from holding food like this.

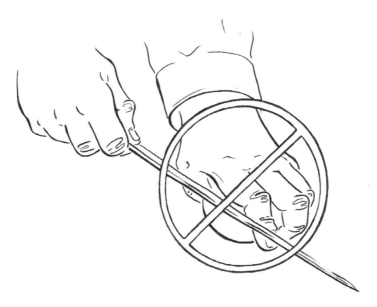

Instead, utilize the "claw grip." This will keep your food steady and your digits clear of sharp objects. Curl your thumb and fingertips in toward your palm and use your knuckles as a guide for the cutting tool.

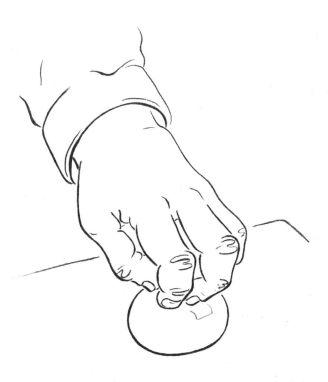

Just the Tip

To prevent roundish fruits and vegetables from wobbling around, cut off the bottom to give yourself a flat base.

Slicing: Although regrettable on a golf course, slicing is absolutely critical for cooking. While resting the tip of your blade on your cutting board, raise the end of the knife closest to the handle. As you slice downward, you should also be thrusting forward—never cut on a backward thrust. In most cases you'll want your slices to be very thin, about ¼ inch.

VideoMark:
Slicing

Chopping: Instead of the slow, measured cuts in a slicing motion, chopping requires quick, vertical whacks. The resultant pieces can be imperfect sizes (about ¼ inches in diameter).

VideoMark:
Chopping

Mincing: Hold the knife so that the edge is facing your chest. Use your free hand to steady the tip of the blade against the cutting board while rocking the heel up and down with the other. The heel should never rise more than an inch or so and the knife should never leave the cutting board. With mincing, the goal is to break whatever you're working with into the tiniest of pieces.

VideoMark:
Mincing

When Things Start Heating Up

Preheating a pan: Preparing a pan for cooking shouldn't feel entirely unfamiliar: Success depends on making sure everything is hot and well-lubricated before introducing your meat.

Put about 1 tablespoon oil in the center of your pan, and then place the pan on the burner. Set the heat to the desired temperature, typically medium to medium-high for sautéing or pan-frying. Rotate the pan so the oil coats the entire base. You'll know it's hot enough when the oil has a shimmering, almost iridescent quality and flows easily when you tilt the pan.

Preheating the oven: Before turning the oven on, take a quick glance to make sure your roommate's pizza from three weeks ago isn't stored inside. This is also a good time to adjust the metal shelves, before it gets hot in there. If your oven doesn't "beep" when it reaches a set temperature, 15 minutes is usually enough time.

Just Enough — The Main Course

Now that you've mastered boiling water and slicing onions, you have all of the skills needed to prepare a delicious meal of boiled sliced onions, which would be a home run if you were trying to woo a 14th-century peasant girl. Unfortunately for both them and you, very few of that demographic survived the bubonic plague. You'll have to step up your game if you want to impress today's antibiotic-rich women.

A balanced meal typically includes a protein (meat, fish, fowl, tofu, etc.), a starch (rice, pasta, potato, etc.) and a vegetable (broccoli, carrots, Larry King, etc.). Additionally, if you're cooking to impress, your finished meal needs to have visual gusto. It is said that people eat with their eyes. In that case, steak with mushroom sauce and potatoes may sound like a classy choice, but visually, your plate would have a depressing wartime palette of browns and grays. This is a meal that makes our eyes think we're eating poo.

Thankfully, we've thought this all through. We'll start by giving you a handful of delicious, visually impressive main entrées, and then follow up with a well-rounded assortment of mix-and-match sides. Your finished product will look and taste complex, but our recipes will require no more than 20 minutes and fourth grade-level reading comprehension.

Blue Balls Beware

Eat, Pray, Masturbate: Food That Will Keep You Single

It's hard to seduce anybody when you look like you just went down on the Jolly Green Giant. Keep vegetable matter out of your teeth by steering clear of:

- Corn on the cob
- Spinach
- Pesto sauce

Aside from stories about cats, nothing is more offensive to the ears than air squeezing its way out of your ass. Avoid untimely methane blasts by limiting:

- Starchy foods
- Dairy
- Carbonated drinks

Just the Tip

The product of your cooking will only be as good as the ingredients used. A pound of all-natural, free-range chicken is better than 2 pounds of hormone-saturated chicken raised in factory-farm squalor. Whenever possible, buy your produce and proteins at farmers' markets or butcher shops. Just be prepared to bend over; decent ingredients don't come cheap.

On-Point Entrées

Grilled Chicken on Sticks

What you tell your date: Grilled Mustard Chicken on Rosemary Skewers with Lemon Crème Fraîche

VideoMark:
Grilled Mustard
Chicken on Rosemary
Skewers with Lemon
Crème Fraîche

This dish is the culinary equivalent of the hot girl with glasses. You're drawn to the assumption that she is unapproachable, out of your league and only dates guys with backstage passes. In reality, she's not complicated at all and has a reputation for being pretty easy. So just like tossing frames on Paris Hilton doesn't magically transform her into Marilyn vos Savant, lancing a few chicken strips with a rosemary sprig doesn't make you Gordon Ramsey. But your date won't know the difference.

You'll have the best presentation if you can score rosemary springs that are 6 to 8 inches long; otherwise you can simply make more skewers from smaller sprigs or just ditch the whole rosemary angle and use standard bamboo or wooden skewers. Make sure your grill or grill pan is nice and hot and lightly oiled before cooking—if you don't hear a sizzle, you jumped the gun. This recipe also makes a knockout dish to bring to cookouts. While all the other dudes are fumbling around with dogs, brats and other harbingers, you'll show up with this proud peacock and win the heart of every babe at the BBQ.

Ingredients:

4 to 6	rosemary sprigs (preferably at least 6 inches long each)
3 tablespoons	Dijon mustard or whole grain mustard
1 tablespoon	fresh lemon juice
1	clove garlic, finely minced
1 teaspoon	salt
½ teaspoon	pepper
2	boneless, skinless chicken breasts
4 to 6	cherry tomatoes

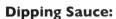

Dipping Sauce:

½ cup crème fraiche (if you can't find crème fraiche you can substitute with sour cream. Do not get low fat.)
1 ½ teaspoons fresh lemon juice
1 teaspoon horseradish or hot sauce
1 tablespoon fresh chives (finely chopped)

Directions:

1. Heat a lightly oiled grill or grill pan to medium-high heat.

2. Rinse the rosemary and pat dry. Pinch your thumb and forefinger just under the very top cluster of needles and pull toward the base of the sprig, leaving the top intact but stripping the rest. Set aside.

3. Mix the ingredients for the dipping sauce in a bowl and set aside.

4. In a separate bowl, whisk the mustard, lemon juice, garlic, salt and pepper together.

5. Cut the chicken into uniform cubes (approximately 1 square inch). Drop into the mustard mixture and toss to coat evenly.

6. Skewer the chicken with the rosemary by stabbing the hard, naked end of the sprig (so many possible jokes) through each cube. Add enough chicken to fill up the skewer without overcrowding, and finish with a cherry tomato.

7. Wash your hands and cutting board to avoid salmonella contamination.

8. Grill the skewers for 4 to 6 minutes, turning with tongs at least once, until cooked through. Serve with the dipping sauce on the side.

Wingmen:

Simple Green Salad with Vinaigrette or Rosemary-Roasted Fingerling Potatoes. (See page 102 for recipes.)

Just the Tip

Make the most of your leftover ingredients. A side of roasted potatoes makes a nice complement to this dish and is a smart use of that extra rosemary. Slice up some of those cherry tomatoes and add them to your salad — let them sit in the dressing for a few minutes to soak up the flavor.

On Good Terms

Mise en place is a French term that loosely translates to "get your shit organized." That is to say, by the time you're ready to start cooking, your garlic should be minced, your onions chopped, your salad greens washed and dried, your seasonings measured, and all of the ingredients and cookware you need within arm's reach. This will set you up for success when it's time to do the actual cooking.

Vegetarian Stir-Fry

What you tell your date: Authentic Vegetarian Stir-Fry

VideoMark:
Authentic Vegetarian
Stir-Fry

If stir-fry were a girl, it'd be a summer fling: something that comes together at the right moment, sizzles intensely for a short period of time, and is over before you know it. It's an excellent meal to make in front of a date because it's all action. You're not obsessively checking the oven or waiting on a pot to boil—you're casually presiding over a blazing pan while being suicide-bombed with hot oil. Though a little patience is required in its preparation (*mise en place* is crucial here), the actual cooking of this dish plays out like the male idea of the perfect coitus: hot, intense and over in less than 10 minutes.

By the way, don't be intimidated by the ingredient list. It may look like a lot of things to acquire, but you need such small amounts that it won't add up to much. Once you get the basic technique down, you can customize it however you want. Though this recipe calls for tofu, you can easily swap it out for beef, chicken, or shrimp.

Ingredients:

8 ounces	extra-firm tofu
1 piece	fresh ginger
8 ounces	fresh shiitake mushrooms
4 ounces	snow peas
2	green onions
	Fresh cilantro leaves
2½ tablespoons	hoisin sauce
1 teaspoon	chili-garlic sauce
1 tablespoon	soy sauce
2 tablespoons	Asian sesame oil

Directions:

1. Drain the tofu and pat dry. Cut into even pieces ½ inch thick by 1 inch long.

2. Peel the ginger with a vegetable peeler. Mince roughly ½ tablespoon worth.

3. Remove the stems from the mushrooms, wipe with a damp paper towel and cut into ¼ inch thick pieces.

4. Rise and dry the snow peas, onions and cilantro. Leave the snow peas whole. Cut the roots off the onions and chop the onions into small pieces. Pick off about ½ cup cilantro leaves.

5. Mix the hoisin, soy and chili-garlic sauces in a bowl with 1 tablespoon water.

6. Heat 1 tablespoon sesame oil in a large nonstick skillet over medium-high heat until shimmering.

7. Add the tofu and cook for 2 to 3 minutes, until golden-brown. Don't overcrowd the pan or the tofu won't crisp up—do it in batches if necessary.

8. Remove the tofu and place in a dish to be added back to the skillet later.

9. Add the remaining 1 tablespoon sesame oil to your skillet. Add the ginger and mushrooms and stir-fry until the mushrooms are tender, about 3 minutes.

10. Add the snow peas, half of the onions and half of the cilantro. Stir-fry for 1 minute.

11. Return the browned tofu to the pan, then stir in the sauce mixture. Sauté until the snow peas are crisp-tender, 1 to 2 minutes.

12. Transfer to a serving bowl and top with the remaining onions and cilantro.

Wingmen:

A side of rice garnished with a small stem of cilantro leaves. Prep all of the vegetables while the rice is cooking; wait until the rice is done to start the stir-fry.

Tossing Your Food

Pan-tossing is a skill that can make for some great showmanship when you're pan-frying, but it should be performed casually, in the flow of your cooking. If you draw too much attention to these sorts of theatrics, it can come off as a little desperate.

This technique works best with a frying pan that has a little lip to it. This will give food a slope to flip off of. You'll also want to make sure your pan is properly lubricated, allowing everything to slide around freely.

1. Firmly grip the handle.

2. Pull the skillet away from the stove and slightly raise the handle, lowering the end of the pan at an angle. The food should be sliding freely downward; if anything is stuck, give your pan a little baby shake.

3. Allow your food to slide down toward the pan's lip. Just before it's about to slide off the pan entirely, raise the handle up and back toward your body in one swift, fluid motion. The flipping will occur during the "pull-back" motion.

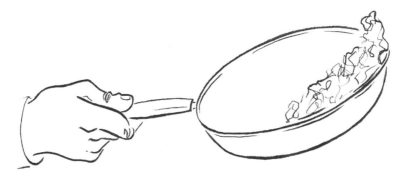

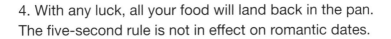

4. With any luck, all your food will land back in the pan. The five-second rule is not in effect on romantic dates.

Pork Chops

What you tell your date: Pan-Roasted Pork Loin Chop with Fennel Crust

VideoMark:
Pan-Roasted
Pork Loin Chop
with Fennel Crust

While there's something undeniably primal about a seared, bone-in piece of pork, the fennel crust suggests a softer sensibility. This is the ideal dish to prepare for the girl who has no shame in admitting her proclivity for a juicy slab of meat. In fact, this meal represents what most guys want in a girl. It's low maintenance, takes under 15 minutes to get ready and looks great.

Ingredients:

2 tablespoons	fennel seeds
2	bone-in pork loin chops, roughly ½ pound each
	Salt
	Pepper
1 tablespoon	extra-virgin olive oil
2	small bunches seedless red grapes (optional)

Directions:

1. Preheat the oven to 375°.

2. Mince the fennel seeds into a rough powder. Alternatively, if you have a coffee grinder, a few seconds in there will do the trick.

3. Season the chops with a pinch of salt and pepper and coat evenly with the fennel.

4. Heat the olive oil (turning to coat the pan) over medium-high heat until it shimmers.

5. Carefully place the chops into the skillet and sear for 2 to 3 minutes until a nice golden-brown crust forms on one side.

6. Flip the chops with a spatula, then transfer the skillet to the oven.

7. Let cook for 8 to 10 minutes.

8. Transfer the chops to a clean plate and let rest for 5 minutes before serving.

Cooking

Wingmen:

Roasted Fingerling Potatoes or Green Beans Almondine.

Take this dish to the next level by placing two small clusters of seedless red grapes (stems attached, 4 to 6 grapes each) in a small baking pan. Lightly coat with olive oil, salt and pepper and throw it in the oven at the same time you add the pork chops. Roughly 15 minutes later (by the time the pork is done resting), your grapes will be nicely roasted. Remove them from the oven and use as garnish for the chops.

Fish in a Bag

What you tell your date: Salmon en Papillote (en pah-pee-YOHT; means "in parchment")

VideoMark:
Salmon en
Papillote

The remarkable thing about this showstopper of a dish is that it fuses a grade-school arts-and-crafts project with a home ec cooking lesson to produce something that looks and tastes like a culinary school student's senior thesis. Though the "en papillote" method produces a crazily succulent piece of fish, it's really set apart by its visual appeal, which allows you to present your date with a gift-wrapped dinner. It's also the definitive Just Enough to Get Laid meal, incorporating cooking, wine, and French in an unstoppable three-pronged attack. Hell, say grace before you eat and you can hit what's known as the Just Enough quadfecta. If it turns out you also built your dining room table with your own hands, even we would consider flying out to your house for a lay.

Ingredients:

2	salmon fillets (6 to 8 ounces each)
	Salt
	Pepper
	Parchment paper (brown preferred, but white will do)
	Extra-virgin olive oil
1	sweet white or yellow onion, thinly sliced
	White wine
1	lemon, thinly sliced
	Dill

Directions:

1. Preheat oven to 450 degrees.

2. Season salmon with salt and pepper.

3. Place two large squares of parchment paper on the counter and fold each in thirds.

4. Smear just a little olive oil in the middle of each piece of parchment. Place some onion slices on the oil, then add the salmon fillets on top. Add a splash of wine to the salmon and top each fillet with 2 lemon slices and a little dill.

5. Now fold the top third and bottom third of the parchment paper over the fish.

6. Seal the ends by tightly twisting them. You should now have something that resembles a Tootsie Roll.

7. Place on a baking sheet and put in the oven to cook for 10 to 12 minutes. To check for doneness, insert a skewer into one of the packages (this one will be yours). If it goes in and out with ease, your fish is cooked. You can also probe with a meat thermometer and remove it when the salmon reaches 125° to 145° (depending on how well done you like your fish).

8. Serve each package on a plate with your sides of choice. Cut an "X" in the center and pull back paper.

Wingmen:

Herbed Rice, Green Beans Almondine or Simple Green Salad with Vinaigrette.

Your Wingmen:

A main course served alone, while satisfying in its own right, will ultimately feel as incomplete as a curling skip without his sweepers. Your title dish definitely requires a couple of culinary sidekicks, and we've got a few stand-outs to choose from. They're not flashy enough to detract from your main dish, but they're robust and filling enough to round out almost any plate.

Simple Green Salad with Vinaigrette

Ingredients:

2 cups	mixed greens
¼ cup	red wine vinegar
1 teaspoon	Dijon mustard
1	clove garlic, minced
¾ cup	extra-virgin olive oil
	Salt

Directions:

1. Rinse the greens in a colander and dry with a paper towel.

2. Pour the vinegar into a medium to large glass bowl and add the mustard and garlic.

3. In a steady stream, pour in the olive oil with one hand while simultaneously whisking with the other until the ingredients have emulsified (combined into one).

4. Whisk in a pinch salt to taste.

5. Transfer the greens to a serving bowl and toss with just enough dressing to coat each leaf.

Green Beans Almondine

Ingredients:

8 ounces	fresh green beans
1 tablespoon	extra-virgin olive oil
1 ounce	sliced almonds

Salt	
Pepper	

Directions:

1. Wash and dry the green beans.

2. In a pan, heat the olive oil over medium heat until shimmering. Drop in the green beans, almonds and a pinch salt and sauté for 5 minutes, until just starting to brown.

3. Cover and cook for another 3 to 5 minutes until crisp and tender.

4. Add a touch of pepper and a little more salt if needed and serve.

Rosemary-Roasted Fingerling Potatoes

Ingredients:

8 ounces	fingerling potatoes
1 tablespoon	extra-virgin olive oil
1 tablespoon	salt
	Pepper
2 tablespoons	minced fresh rosemary

Directions:

1. Preheat the oven to 450°.

2. Wash and dry the potatoes.

3. Mince about two tablespoons of fresh rosemary.

4. Put the potatoes in a baking dish and toss with the olive oil to coat. Add the salt, pepper and rosemary and toss again to coat evenly.

5. Bake for about 25 minutes or until the potatoes can be pierced easily with a fork.

Herbed Rice

Ingredients:

1¾ cups	water
1 cup	white rice
	Salt
1 tablespoon	unsalted butter
Handful	finely minced fresh herbs (chives, thyme, parsley)

Directions:

1. Add the water, rice and a pinch salt to a pot and bring to a boil, uncovered, over high heat.

2. Once boiling, give the rice a quick stir to make sure it isn't sticking, then cover and reduce heat to medium-low.

3. Let simmer for 20 minutes, then remove from the heat and let sit for 5 minutes. Keep covered the entire time.

4. Remove the cover, add the butter and herbs and fluff the rice with a fork.

Note: Both the rice and potatoes take longer to cook than your main dishes *and* will stay hot for quite a while if covered. Avoid the stress of multitasking by preparing them first.

View from a Broad

"A guy who can cook is a provider. It means he can take care of me, which secretly, all women still want."
Karen S., Dundalk, MD

A Sure Thing — Just Desserts

Sweet foods like chocolate and fruit have long been considered aphrodisiacs, although there's no real hard evidence to support this. But the correlation between dessert and sex is definitely there. That's why people often incorporate whipped cream and chocolate into their bedroom antics, but rarely figure out a way to slot in flank steak or curried eggplant. It's also why condoms are flavored in chocolate and vanilla, but never cabbage or codfish.

Having said that, we don't really recommend making yourself a dessert. A whipped cream banana hammock is disgusting, and scraggly pubes do not make for a good garnish. Keep dessert and sex sequential, but don't try to combine the two or you'll end up having both of them by yourself.

Flaming Bananas

VideoMark:
Flaming Bananas

Cooking

No, Flaming Bananas is not the name of a gay bar—we're literally setting fruit on fire. Such pyrotechnics make this delicious dish a fitting grand finale, but be forewarned: This concoction is as unstable as Lindsay Lohan. The dessert carries Machiavellian power best compared to a piece of sexual plutonium. Successfully harnessing the raw energy from the Flaming Bananas can lead to your date unpeeling her clothes. Being careless, however, can lead to a blow job of the unpleasant variety—the one where fire blows up in your face.

Blue Balls Beware

Avoid a culinary catastrophe by using your head—the one on top of your shoulders.

Tools:

frying pan, long reach lighter (or a long match)

Ingredients:

2	bananas, peeled
6 tablespoons	unsalted butter
¼ cup	dark brown sugar
¼ cup	dark rum
	Vanilla ice cream

Directions:

1. Peel your bananas and slice them into ¼-inch-wide pieces.

2. Melt the butter and brown sugar in a skillet. Add the bananas and sauté until tender.

3. Remove the skillet from the heat and pour in the rum. Take a shot for yourself to verify the quality.

4. Be extremely cautious here. Holding the pan away from anything flammable (like your date and your eyebrows), carefully ignite the rum with a long reach lighter or long match. Use a non-wooden, long-handled spoon to baste the bananas with the burning rum until the flame peters out.

5. Scoop the vanilla ice cream into bowls. Place the bananas on top of the ice cream. Drizzle the remaining rum mixture in the pan over the ice cream.

Mint Chocolate Mousse

VideoMark:
Mint Chocolate
Mousse

Chocolate mousse has a lot going for it. It's simultaneously light and rich, airy and creamy. And on the aphrodisiac scale, it ranks just under "Barry White reading a scene from *The Notebook*." This version gets even more points for leaving you and your date minty fresh and make-out ready.

Ingredients:

⅔ cups	chocolate chips
¾ cups	heavy cream
¼ teaspoon	pure vanilla extract
¼ teaspoon	mint extract
2 to 4	mint leaves

Directions:

1. Heat the chocolate and half of the cream over low heat until the chocolate is melted. Add the vanilla and mint extract. Cook for a few minutes until the mixture is smooth and creamy. Remove from the heat and let cool.

2. In a large, chilled bowl, beat the remaining cream with a whisk until stiff peaks begin to form.

3. Once the chocolate mixture has cooled close to room temperature, beat it into the whipped cream until peaks start to form.

4. Spoon the mousse into a wine or martini glass and garnish with the mint leaves. This can be served immediately or made ahead and refrigerated (covered) for up to 24 hours.

Just the Tip

Don't go overboard on portions. Inundating your date with a Cheesecake Factory-sized mammoth dessert will just lead to bloated sloth, which is not the deadly sin you're interested in.

The "Morning After" Omelet

VideoMark:
The "Morning After" Omelet

An omelet the morning after functions both as a classy way to replenish depleted protein and as an opportunity to prove that the skills you exhibited in the kitchen last night were more than a flash in the pan. Although fairly easy and ridiculously cheap to make, the omelet benefits from its reputation as one of the hallmarks of classic French cuisine, commanding a respect most breakfast items can only dream of. Just go to any buffet and you'll get the picture: The guy with the omelet pan sports a 24-inch toque, while everyone else rocks a hairnet.

This particular recipe calls for chives and Gruyère (a French cow's-milk cheese), but any mild, good-melting cheese will suffice. Serve with a simple side salad and a couple of mimosas (1 part orange juice, 2 parts sparkling wine), queue up a little Django Reinhardt and you'll be treating her to the kind of brunch most city dwellers enthusiastically shell out $20 and endure a 45-minute wait to experience. Follow it up with couple more mimosas and you may get the chance to prove that the skills you exhibited in the bedroom last night were no fluke either.

66 99 Quintessential Quotation

"Nothing would be more tiresome than eating and drinking if God had not made them a pleasure as well as a necessity."

— *Voltaire*

Ingredients:

2	large or extra-large eggs
1½ tablespoons	chopped fresh chives
1 tablespoon	water
	Salt
	Pepper
1 tablespoon	butter
3 tablespoons	grated Gruyère cheese

Directions:

1. Preheat the oven to 200°.

2. Heat a pan over medium-high heat.

3. While your pan is heating, grate the cheese and chop the chives. Whisk the eggs, 1 tablespoon chives, the water and a pinch salt and pepper in a bowl until the yolks and whites are combined.

4. When the skillet is hot, spray it well with nonstick cooking spray (like Pam) and drop in the butter. Swirl it around to coat.

5. Pour in the egg mixture. Using a heatproof spatula (or the back of a fork), gently scramble the eggs using small, circular motions until curds start to form, 30 to 60 seconds.

6. As the mixture firms, hold some egg back from the side and tilt the pan, letting the uncooked eggs run to the bottom.

7. Cook for another 30 seconds or so, until cooked through but not dried out.

8. Scatter the cheese evenly, leaving a thin outer perimeter uncovered (like you were topping a pizza).

9. Fold one-third of the omelet over toward the center. Tilt the pan over a plate so that a third of the other side hangs over the edge. Using your spatula to guide the omelet, invert the pan so the omelet flips over itself. Garnish with the remaining chives.

10. Put this omelet in the oven to keep warm while you make hers.

Just the Tip

This recipe works best if using a smaller (6 to 8 inch) skillet, otherwise your omelet may look a little thin. If you don't have any pans that small, make one large 4 egg omelette and share it. A pan with a non-stick surface is greatly preferred if you want to avoid making impromptu scrambled eggs.

If you're already making omelets for two, of course, then you've already witnessed firsthand the seductive powers of cooking. There's an old proverb that states: "Give a man a fish and you will feed him for a day. Teach a man to fish and you will feed him for a lifetime." They forgot to add that if you show that man how to skillfully prepare his fish, you can also get him laid pretty consistently. Cooking can satisfy your appetite, your creativity—and, if you play your carbs right, your libido.

Religion

Not Quite Enough — Rules to Live By

Almost Enough — Plot & Cast of Characters

Just Enough — Dating & Religion

A Sure Thing — Tantra & Kama Sutra

*D*on't think that by reading this chapter, you'll be absolved of any sins. In fact, you'll probably be committing one. Why do you think whores sweat in church? Yes, it could be due to herpes flare-ups, but it's more likely caused by the encroaching heat from hell. Mixing religion and sex is a combustible cocktail that should be avoided in most cases. But since the typical guy would gladly sell his soul to the devil for just one night in Paris (Hilton), we're going to teach you enough about religion to attract your own devoted followers, so you can sell your soul for something else.

Pastor Joel Osteen is able to attract more than 7 million followers each week. So what do you need to know about religion to attract just one person? As it turns out, you don't need to preach to a choir; you just need to avoid offending your date's religious sensibilities.

Consider this all-too-common occurrence: You've been impressing a girl all night with your finest witticisms, when suddenly the topic of religion pops up and you say the wrong thing. The date instantly unravels; your status plummets from "charming potential sex partner" to "Antichrist," and suddenly the odds are stacked against you. Revealing yourself as a mortal enemy of God can really compromise your chances of getting into heaven on earth.

Of course, religion isn't guaranteed to get you thumping anything other than bibles. Even Ted Haggard had to pay for it. But there's definitely something to be said about learning enough about religion so that you can find your Virgin Mary (or Jenny.) We're going to give you a scriptural history that's easier to digest than a communion wafer or kosher frank. Then we'll cover some basic religious ground rules and dating the devout. And if that's not enough, we'll let Hinduism guide us toward the path to spiritual satisfaction so that you and your date might both share in a little Bootyism—and so that you'll be capable of pleasing her as if blessed with the four arms of Vishnu.

Although none of this information will save your soul from eternal damnation, it should be enough to save your Saturday nights from eternal frustration. And if this minimal effort gets you laid, eternal damnation is a small price to pay. Amen.

 The Bare Necessities

Everything is optional, so pick and choose at your discretion: framed photographs of loved ones, religious texts (Old and New Testament, the Talmud, Koran, Tao Te Ching, *The God Delusion*), Kama Sutra mat.

Not Quite Enough — Rules to Live By

If you're already bending a girl's dating standards, it's only fair that you avoid offending her moral standards. And really, toeing the line between good and evil isn't all that complicated. Most religious structures of morality are neatly encapsulated by the Golden Rule: "Do unto others as you would have them do unto you." We've broken down what this entails into 10 mostly universal religious regulations—because the last thing you want to do is insult the guiding moral compass of the woman with whom you're trying to get sacrilegious.

Religion

1. Don't Kill Thy Neighbor

Hopefully this doesn't radically upset your current lifestyle, but murder is absolutely verboten. This applies even if you're trying to nap and somewhere outside DJ Jazzy Jerk-off is assaulting you with his SUV's military-grade stereo system.

2. No Five-Finger Discounts

Except for downloading music and stealing Wi-Fi. If you're dumb enough to leave your connection unsecured, even God would consider it fair game if He was desperate enough to update His Twitter account.

3. Don't Make Shit Up

You should try your best not to bear false witness, unless a girl asks an obvious trap question like, "How do I look?" or "Do you find my sister attractive?"

4. Refrain from Strange

Respect the boundaries of relationships, both your own and other people's. So no matter how single you are, you shouldn't do your buddy's girlfriend. And even when they break up, she's still off-limits for at least a couple of weeks.

5. Send a Mother's Day Card

Your mother schlepped you around in her stomach for nine months before you destroyed her body with an *Alien*-esque delivery. The least you can do is call her from time to time. Anybody who changed your diaper when you were a baby deserves the same favor returned when she becomes senile.

6. Take a Day Off

Whether you call it the Sabbath or just football Sunday, it's important to take a break from work to spend time with your family and your girlfriend. If you put your job ahead of her, it's the only type of job you're ever bound to receive.

7. Don't Say "Goddamn It"

Only your date is allowed to defile God's name, and that's only when you've been able to perform an act of God.

8. Jealousy Is a Bitch

There's an old saying: "Jealousy is the only vice that gives no pleasure." If you are going to sin, you should at least get something out of it.

9. Give Props to the Man Upstairs

Whomever your date prays to in a monotheistic religion, he is the one true God. If she finds you worshipping the false Idols determined by Ryan Seacrest, she's bound to question more than just your religious fervor.

10. You Can't Take It with You

It's said that money is the root of all evil, but then again, not having money is the root of being single. The takeaway is not to dedicate your life entirely to the church of the almighty dollar. Believe it or not, the dollar is worth even less in heaven than the Canadian dollar is in America.

Almost Enough — Plot & Cast of Characters

If we studied religious texts as closely as we watched our favorite films, we'd all have master's degrees in not going to hell. Most of us know more about the singer Madonna than the biblical Madonna; more about Luke Skywalker than Luke the apostle. And the only reason we can name each of the seven deadly sins is because we've seen *Seven*. It's not like this is surprising. Cinema is designed to entertain, engage and sometimes arouse, while religious texts are bogged down with weighty prose and arcane regulations. We're going to make it easier to parse the narratives in the Judeo-Christian-Islamic tradition by interpreting them as a series of films. Think of these films like the *Passion of the Christ*, but much more condensed and without the erotic overtones or Mel Gibson-esque tirades.

The God the Father Trilogy
Created by: Yahweh/God/Allah

God the Father Part I: The Hebrew Bible (Judaism/Christianity)

Written/directed by: Moses
Co-written by: Joshua
Starring: Abraham, Isaac, Jacob, Joseph
Supporting cast: Adam, Eve, David, Solomon
Lead set designer: Noah

Plot synopsis: Moses' stirring 1200 BC directorial debut begins with Yahweh (aka God) hanging out by himself in the dark, bored out of his mind. He creates the world and two people, Adam and Eve, who promptly disobey His command in an unfortunate fruit mix-up (which ensures the fall of mankind). But their eventual descendent Abraham makes a covenant with Yahweh, who promises to bestow upon him numerous progeny and eventually some nice real estate in Israel. This same covenant is passed down to Abraham's son Isaac, and then to Isaac's son Jacob, who brings the flock to Egypt, where they're regrettably enslaved by their son Joseph for a couple of centuries.

Enter Moses. He leads them out of Egypt and into the Promised Land of Israel. Through Yahweh, Moses establishes laws that eventually coalesce into Judaism, which bases its faith around the worship of a single deity—unlike all the competing polytheistic religions. And Yahweh is tentatively pleased.

God the Father Part 2: The New Testament (Christianity)

Directed by: Paul
Written by: Matthew, Mark, Luke and John
Starring: Jesus, Mary
Supporting cast: John the Baptist, 12 Apostles, Herod and Pilate, Joseph
Special effects by: Jesus

Plot synopsis: The much-anticipated sequel is a riveting biopic of Jesus. It's the year 0001. The blessed Abrahamic bloodline has continued to flow through the generations all the way down to Jesus, who is birthed by Mary. But there's a twist. His father? God himself, which makes Jesus both the Messiah and the Son of God. After a semi-successful carpenter gig, Jesus begins following his true calling: preaching loving thy enemy and thy neighbor alike. He buttresses these speaking engagements with several charming miracles, and begins accumulating adherents and critics alike. Among his enemies is the Roman government. They call for his execution, and he's hanged on the cross. However, three days later, Jesus pops back to life for one last farewell tour. He ambles around Israel for 40 days and then ascends to heaven.

Needless to say, with this miraculous death-defying feat, the Son of God accumulates more than a few more adherents. Paul helps bring Jesus' doctrine together as a faith, codifying the rules that distinguish it from its birth in Judaism.

Religion

God the Father Part 3: The Koran (Islam)

Written/directed by: Mohammed
Starring: Mohammed
Supporting cast: The Four Caliphs, Fatima

Plot synopsis: It's the seventh century, well into the future. Christianity has surged, becoming the region's dominant religion. Meanwhile, in Arabia, the visionary prophet Mohammed declares that he is a descendant of Ishmael and is receiving revelations from God (now going by the alias Allah), which will continue throughout the rest of his life. He preaches these revelations first to his trusted companions, and then gradually to the Arabian people at large. The message thrives despite prosecution, eventually solidifying into Islam (which is based on the prophet's revelations as transcribed in the Koran).

Muslims believe the original Biblical texts were authentic revelations, and that both Jesus and Moses were true prophets. But they also believe those antiquated texts were corrupted over time, and have thereby been replaced by the divinely inspired Koran (which is the verbatim word of God). Islam shares a lot of similarities with the Jewish and Christian traditions, but is distinguished by, among other things, the five primary religious duties known as the Pillars of Islam.

Epilogue: The three Abrahamic religions, united by their shared history and analogous core beliefs, came together to establish a new world order of peaceful harmony.

Just Enough — Dating & Religion

On the surface, dating and religion seem to go together as well as peanut butter and razor blades. The whole sacred subject is like a ticking time bomb, and inadvertently offending her faith can abolish any chance you might have had of getting to know her biblically. On the other hand, demonstrating sensitivity to her religion will give you more than a snowball's chance in hell of getting some use out of your divining rod. And this doesn't entail wholesale life changes like converting your tool shed into a church or eliminating ham sandwiches from your diet—you just need to briefly educate yourself about some of what to expect on a date.

Judaism

Breaking Bread

Before you make reservations for dinner with that cute chick from JDate, remember that not all foods are kosher (the Jewish law that prohibits eating pig products, shellfish, or anything that mixes meat with dairy). If she's into Jewish orthodoxy, this means you should avoid taking her out for lobster, bacon, cheeseburgers, or bacon-cheeseburger-stuffed lobsters.

Meeting Her Makers

If you aren't Jewish, you're facing an up-Mount Sinai battle when it comes to schmoozing her 'rents. Some mothers want nothing more than for their daughters to meet a nice Jewish boy, get married in a synagogue, and have a bounty of Jewish babies. You'll need to win points by being respectful. The period from sundown on Friday to sundown on Saturday is knows as Shabbat. During this period, Orthodox Jews have a formal dinner, do not turn on or off electricity, and refrain from working. If they have lights on, do not turn them off. If somebody is wearing a yarmulke, don't be a schmuck and try to throw it like a Frisbee.

Pilgrimage to Her Holy Land

Traditional Judaism prohibits sexual activity before marriage. It even goes so far as to expressly prohibit lewd thoughts, which on the surface might seem like trying to prohibit water from being wet. The key here is that the less orthodox a woman is, the more liberal her attitudes will be toward sex. So if you're looking to turn "spin the dreidel" into "spin the bottle," your best bet might be to look for Sarah Silverman.

Christianity

Breaking Bread

Your options are pretty wide open here, as the Christian faith doesn't restrict much in the way of diet. Christians who observe Lent (Catholics, Orthodox, and Anglicans/Episcopalians) don't eat meat on Fridays during that time, but that's, like, six days a year. And even then, fish is fine to eat. Take her out to a seafood restaurant during this time, or take her out to a steakhouse and just politely ask her to wait in the car.

Meeting Her Makers

 Christian parents can run the gamut from strict drill sergeants to devil-may-care nontraditionalists. It's a real Christly crapshoot. Most will prefer a lack of sexual contact in their presence, but it's preposterous to imagine any denomination of parent who encourages dinnertime handjobs. Best thing to do is play it safe and be respectful—bow your head slightly and close your eyes if they say grace, and at all costs avoid religious or political debate. Family will probably be a priority in their lives, so being invited over to their home in the first place is a pretty good sign that they don't consider you an Antichrist.

Pilgrimage to Her Holy Land

 More conservative Christians (especially Catholics) require waiting until marriage to have sex, which might explain why some rush to marriage a decade or two before they're really ready for it. This policy varies greatly depending on the girl, however, but no matter what, you should at least pretend that you don't treat sex as a trivial pleasure.

❝❞
Quintessential Quotation

"When his life was ruined, his family killed, his farm destroyed, Job knelt down on the ground and yelled up to the heavens, 'Why god? Why me?' and the thundering voice of God answered, 'There's just something about you that pisses me off."

—Stephen King

125

Islam

Breaking Bread

The flesh of a pig is considered unclean in the Islamic faith, and some strict Muslims do not eat animals that have been killed in varied and sundry ways (strangling, violent blows, etc).

Meeting Her Makers

Traditionally, Islam does not allow dating at all, even between Muslims. If you still want to proceed, realize that before you can flirt with a girl, you should expect to court her father first. Compliment him on the beauty of his wife and daughters, but do not directly address the women in the home. Also, eat everything in sight. Muslims make hospitality a priority and will appreciate your receptivity. Islam also requires that chaperones be present at all times when unmarried members of the opposite sex hang out socially.

Pilgrimage to Her Holy Land

Sex with a girl from a conservative Muslim family is a hard one to pull off. In fact, it's basically impossible, as Islam prohibits all sex before marriage.

Religion

126

Hinduism/Buddhism

Breaking Bread

Hindus often view cattle as sacred, so will generally avoid eating steak. Both Hinduism and Buddhism often consider the Karma of food they eat, and vegetarians are quite common. Depending on the girl's cultural background, you should probably anticipate a preference for ball-hair-searing spiciness.

Meeting Her Makers

Meeting the parents of a Hindu or Buddhist girl is often complicated by cultural, as opposed to religious, differences. Many won't be thrilled by the idea of their children dating outside of their faith or race, but this can often be overcome. Otherwise, don't drink/smoke/eat excessively in their presence, and keep aggressive political opinions to yourself.

Pilgrimage to Her Holy Land

Even though the Hindis literally wrote the book on sex, depending on the sect, premarital relations are sometimes frowned upon. Buddhism, lacking a supreme God, is pretty tolerant of it. But both religions frown on overindulgence, so moderation in sex is implied. If you get carried away with these sorts of bodily impulses, you run the risk of being reincarnated as a crap animal like a roach, or a syphilis bacteria.

A Sure Thing —Tantra & Kama Sutra

As much as there is to learn from the Judeo-Christian-Islamic tradition, all of these religions tend to be somewhat withholding in the sex-tip department. They spend a great deal of time describing *what* a sin is, but they completely gloss over *how to* sin. Hinduism is like the *Cosmopolitan* of religions, going into great detail about how to achieve better, more fulfilling orgasms—especially when it comes to Tantra and Kama Sutra. These are off-shoot Hindu practices, more akin to a spiritual experience than a religious ceremony (like Native Americans smoking their peace pipes.) They approach sex not as a sin, but as a means of getting closer with your Supreme being(s), while proving that the Golden Rule is as apropos in the bedroom as it is in the temple. Sex is all about reciprocation, and selfish lovers are doomed to a life of seclusion.

Tantra

When we think of Tantra, we probably think of Sting and his marathon sexual sessions, and his claims of orgasms lasting longer than his concerts. Actually, though, sex is a small slice of the Tantric pie. Tantra is really more of a system of beliefs and practices guiding you down the spiritual path to reincarnation, and using it simply to achieve raunchier sexcapades is antithetical to its intent. But we're sure you don't care about that, so we're going to disregard the spiritual path and focus on the path to sexual bliss.

On Good Terms

Yoni: Sanskrit for a woman's sacred temple (also known as her vagina).

Lingam: Sanskrit for the male phallus (penis).

Chakra: Focal points of energy in the body where psychic forces and bodily functions interact.

Religion

How to Perform Sat Kriya

Sat Kriya is like a car key for the reckless, out-of-control vehicle known as your sex drive. It allows you to rechannel sexual impulses to achieve creativity and healing, but can also raise your overall sexual energy and help quell your fears of inadequacies as a lover.

I. Sit with your heels tucked underneath your butt and your back straight.

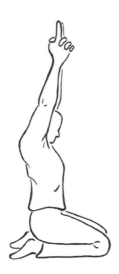

2. Stretch your arms straight up against your ears, keeping your elbows straight. Your hands should be intertwined except for your index fingers, which should be pointing straight up and pressed together like a bad Charlie's Angels pose.

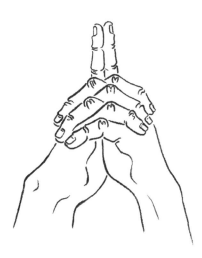

3. Gently stretch your spine straight up to the sky while elongating your neck. Your spine and neck should form one straight line.

4. It's time to chant. In a powerful voice, chant "sat" while you bring your naval inward toward the spine. Then, in a softer voice, chant "nam" as you relax your naval outward. The rest of your body should remain as still as possible.

5. Continue the "sat nam" contraction at a steady pace—slightly slower than once per second. Do this for about three minutes, or until you're bored.

6. After your sat nam contractions, end the exercise by inhaling deeply and applying **root lock**, **diaphragm lock**, and **neck lock**. Imagine these locks are bringing energy through your spine and into your brain. Now exhale. You can repeat this three times for maximum brain energy.

 On Good Terms

Root lock: Contract your butt, kegel and lower naval muscles.

Diaphragm lock: Pull in your diaphragm.

Neck lock: Pull your neck muscles back while tucking in your chin.

7. And on the seventh step, you rest. Lie on your back for however long you performed this exercise and meditate on the renewed sexual vigor reverberating through your body.

VideoMark:
How to Perform
Sat Kriya

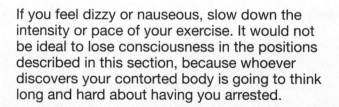

Blue Balls Beware

If you feel dizzy or nauseous, slow down the intensity or pace of your exercise. It would not be ideal to lose consciousness in the positions described in this section, because whoever discovers your contorted body is going to think long and hard about having you arrested.

Kama Sutra

Kama Sutra calls to mind titillating images of impassioned couples bending themselves into various alphabet shapes. Again, though, as with Tantra, this is a bit of a mischaracterization—Kama Sutra is really more concerned with how to use our sexuality as a means for spiritual fulfillment—not that this precludes teaching us some pretty remarkable positions. Reading over this, you may even find you know more about Hinduism than you originally thought—because you've been inadvertently practicing some of these positions for years. Now let's imagine what they'd be like if there were actually another person in the room.

Just the Tip

If a woman says she's "spiritual but not religious," this is code for "easy," and sexuality can be openly discussed. On the other hand, if a woman says she is "religious but not spiritual," then she's just a pain in the ass.

On Good Terms

Dharma: More than simply the mysterious organization in *Lost*, in Hinduism and Buddhism, Dharma represents the essential principles of natural law. And unlike *Lost*, Hinduism and Buddhism do not try to leave you more confused than when you began.

Artha: The acquisition of arts, land, gold, cattle, wealth and friends. It is further the protection of what is acquired, and the increase of what is protected.

Kama: Enjoyment of the five senses. Hearing, feeling, seeing, tasting and smelling assisted by the mind together with the soul.

Religion

Sexual Compatibility

Kama Sutra views males and females as each falling into three distinct categories. If you're male, you're either a rabbit, bull or horse. If you're a woman, you're either a doe, cow or she-elephant. Do not actually call your date a she-elephant, or the only position you'll find yourself in is hunched over the sink trying to wash the mace out of your eyes.

View from a Broad

"A guy having faith is a turn-on to me. It shows he can commit."

Renee, Boston, MA

The categories are determined in a pretty simple fashion: by the size of your lingam and the depth of your date's yoni. Check the chart to see if the two of you are compatible. Of course, by the time you've discovered the depth of your date's yoni, you probably won't be too worried about whether or not you're compatible enough to screw. This is really more of a guide to long-term sexual fulfillment between you and your she-elephant.

Size Matters

Men

Here's how to find your lingam animal: First, go ahead and measure your erect penis (we'll pretend that you don't already know this measurement to the millimeter). Then compare your measurements to the chart below:

> **Hare:** around 4.5 inches
> **Bull:** around 6.75 inches
> **Horse:** around 9 inches

The vast majority of us will fall in range of the bullpen(is), but a smaller percentage will find themselves with hares or horses. Neither rules out satisfying lovemaking sessions— you just need to find the appropriate partner.

If you find your supposed Horse dong is suspiciously adequate for your date's Mare snare, you probably need to reexamine your tape measure. That also explains why your Magnum condoms fit like a broomstick in a Hefty bag.

Men

Hare   Bull   Horse

Women

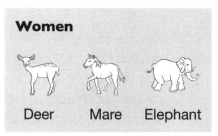

Deer   Mare   Elephant

Size

Equal

Not Equal

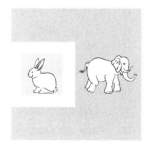

Positions

We've selected some of the hottest and/or most awkward sexual positions in the Kama Sutra. The goal isn't necessarily about achieving orgasm—it's about indulging in all your senses, about not overlooking a single square inch of your lover's body. Sex is about exploration, and the Kama Sutra is your GPS.

The Oily Refinery

Your partner should lie on her back with her feet in the air, as if she were doing a naked sit-up. Meanwhile, shimmy in front of her and slide your ass up her legs until you've got an appropriate vantage from which to strike. Actual penetration will be harder than landing the plane at midnight *Top Gun*, but once you've made contact there's very little hard work ahead of you. Just remember that she'll be in a Cirque du Soleil contortion and may not have your endurance (for once).

The Crab Cake

You and your partner should be sitting across from one another, legs akimbo. "Crab walk" toward each other by marching your buttocks forward in military fashion—left, right, left, right. Once you're touching, congratulations: You are now having sex. Hopefully. Glance downward to confirm that this is the case. And pray you don't lose your balance and start tipping backwards; you're liable to break a bone(r).

The Damp Scarf

As your partner is lying back on the bed with her toes touching, thread your neck through her legs. Your pelvises should be at roughly the same height, so proceed as you normally would. Ideally, she'll be capable of being completely suspended from your neck. This is a great position if the two of you have been sitting down all day and need to stretch your legs.

Stand and Deliver

Stand behind your date and pick her up by her buttocks. If you're not a professional bodybuilder and she weighs more than 80 pounds, you might find it easier to allow her legs to be supported by the bed. Once you've gotten hold of her, maneuver her onto your lap. Now you just need to be mindful of not dropping her and not allowing your knees to buckle. If your balance is upset, one or more of you is going to fall to the floor, and we don't know of any Kama Sutra position that involves a broken arm.

Astronomy

Not Quite Enough — Finding the North Star

Almost Enough — Planet Spotting

Just Enough — Constellations

A Sure Thing — Astrology 101

S ay what you will about nerdy astronomers, but Galileo fathered three illegitimate children, Aristotle had two wives plus a concubine, and Stephen Hawking had an affair with his nurse while confined to a wheelchair. We're pretty sure it wasn't his R2-D2 voice box that got him laid; it was his intimate knowledge of celestial bodies.

Since you probably don't know your ass from Uranus, you've been deprived of countless opportunities for a Big Bang. Think about it for a second. At the end of a date, isn't the goal to get a woman on her back alone in the dark? Knowing a little astronomy gives you a reason to start the date there. Stargazing is a tried-and-true seduction technique practiced since ancient times. Johannes Kepler once said, "Astronomy is the second most fun thing you can do in the dark with a woman and your index finger."[1]

---

[1] Okay, Johannes Kepler did not say this…but that doesn't mean it isn't true.

There are many other valid reasons for acquiring a little heavenly knowledge. Ancient Egyptians used the stars to position their pyramids, and Druids erected Stonehenge to measure the seasons. Once you finish reading this chapter, you'll be able to sort out the inky confusion of the nighttime sky and become confidently capable of navigating heaven and earth using only the North Star.

We'll also teach you a little soft-core astronomy that will prepare you to spot several planets and a few kick-ass constellations. And yes, by demonstrating all of this knowledge, you'll be properly equipped to navigate the sea of stars and retain an excellent chance of probing the dark side of your date.

If all the astronomical science isn't enough, we'll also touch upon rudimentary astrology—which itself is a rudimentary pseudo-scientific understanding of reality. Whether or not you believe in magical stars forecasting your own inevitability is insignificant. There are plenty of girls who love it and believe in romantic destiny. Read on, and we'll help you answer the inevitable question "What's your sign?" without unwittingly forfeiting any chance for getting a little Vagittarius. One way or the other, whether you're using a horoscope or a telescope, the stars can ensure you get laid more than once in a blue moon.

The Bare Necessities

A blanket, a starry night, a girl, your index finger, a black hole, astronaut ice cream.

Not Quite Enough — Finding the North Star

Before Google Maps, MapQuest or gas station attendants, stars were the most reliable way to navigate from point A to point B. Many MapQuest users actually maintain that simply throwing sticks in the air and observing their patterns is a more accurate way to find an address. Celestial navigation's proverbial "search" button begins with the North Star, also called Polaris.

It's the most common navigational star because it lines up directly with Earth's axis of rotation right above the North Pole. That means once you locate Polaris, you can find your way on the ground or track down other constellations in the sky. And correctly locating north is the first step toward navigating your way down south on the celestial body stargazing by your side.

1. To find the North Star, start by locating one of the most recognizable star patterns in the sky, the Big Dipper. It's that iconic formation of seven bright stars that resemble a huge soup ladle. Depending on the time of year, it may appear upside down, as if drunkenly spilling soup on the rest of the galaxy.

2. Now draw a line between the two stars located at the end of the Big Dipper's bowl. Follow this line upward from the bottom of the bowl about five times the line's length. There you'll find the handle of the Little Dipper.

3. Not only have you found your second star pattern, you've just found Polaris—it's at the very tip of the Little Dipper's handle. Wherever you are, this star very nearly approximates the direction of due north, so it's the perfect stargazing starting point. Good job, Copernicus. You've figured out the way to Canada.

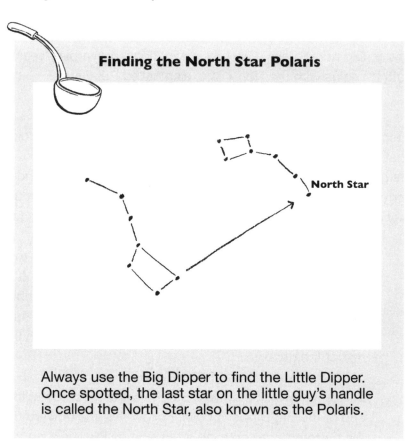

Finding the North Star Polaris

North Star

Always use the Big Dipper to find the Little Dipper. Once spotted, the last star on the little guy's handle is called the North Star, also known as the Polaris.

Dropping Knowledge

In 2010, it was reported that 300 sextillion stars were discovered in our galaxy.

On Good Terms

Asterism: A pattern of stars, often part of a formal constellation. Strictly speaking, the Big and Little Dippers are not constellations—they're asterisms.

Ursa Major: The Big Dipper forms the backbone of the constellation Ursa Major, or the Great Bear.

Ursa Minor: The Little Dipper and Ursa Minor (or Smaller Bear) share the same seven stars, which really illustrates the flexibility of these star formations. The same handful of stars can either depict a little utensil for serving soup or a ferocious predator.

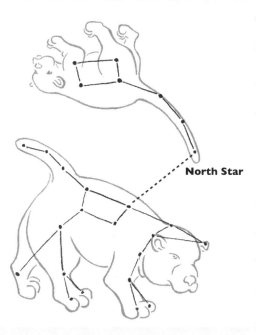

North Star

145

Almost Enough — Planet Spotting

There are up to six planets potentially visible without a telescope: Jupiter, Mars, Mercury, Saturn, Uranus and Venus. Spotting Mercury or Uranus, however, is almost as hard as finding a G-spot in a haystack. That's especially unfortunate, because we would have made at least half a dozen Uranus/your-anus jokes. We'll do our best to still take a few pokes at Uranus.

We've assembled a short summertime guide for tracking down the other four "naked eye" planets: Jupiter, Mars, Saturn and Venus. Seeing them in person from Earth is a little like seeing a sold-out arena concert from the cheap seats—too small and blurry to really make out any details, but with a little booze, it'll still be a damn good show.

Jupiter

Like Kanye West, Jupiter (named after the mythological Roman king of gods) is comprised of more hot air than almost any other object in our solar system. The two also share the unique ability of taking up tons of time and space while lacking any real solid substance. At least Jupiter doesn't have a Twitter account.

Mars

Named after the Roman god of war, Mars, known as the Red Planet, is easily recognizable by its distinctive bright coloration, which unfortunately comes from the presence of iron oxide (rust) and not rivers of blood. Water ice has been confirmed on the surface, which makes Mars a good candidate for the discovery of microbial life, not to mention a refreshing summer getaway destination.

Saturn

Saturn, like Jupiter, is made mostly of gas, as if it just got back from a Chipotle run. The name comes from the Titan god who was replaced by Jupiter—so Saturn is like MySpace to Jupiter's Facebook. Pluto is Friendster—nobody ever gave a shit about Pluto. Saturn is also the planet everyone associates with its rings, which are sadly not visible with the naked eye. Though it's probably a good thing your date doesn't start thinking about rings.

Astronomy

In 2006, astronomers got together and officially gave Pluto the bad news: It was being kicked out of the planetary system and receiving a demotion to dwarf planet status. Calling Pluto a planet today sounds as dated as referring to Pamela Anderson as hot.

Venus

Venus is the brightest object in the night sky after the moon, which explains why it's named after the Roman goddess of beauty. If we had to have sex with one planet, Venus would be a close second behind Uranus. It's a brilliant white (some claim it has a slightly bluish tint) and is always close to the horizon at sunrise or sunset.

Spotting the Planets

1. Wait Until Summer

There are definitely visible planets during the winter months, but stargazing in January can cause blue balls from both the unromantic frigid air and from actual hypothermia. We've structured this section around the more outdoor-friendly summer months of June, July and August.

2. Find Polaris

Using the steps outlined in the Not Quite Enough section, figure out which direction is north. If nothing else, it'll be impressive that you can do this without the aid of your phone's GPS.

Astronomy

3. Find the East-West Horizon Line

As you're facing Polaris, to your right will lie the east and to your left the west. You'll need to be facing a particular direction depending on the month, so establishing which horizons are north, east, south and west will make your life a lot easier.

 View from a Broad

"There's something about staring at a night sky. It's not just romantic. It's primal. It unleashes our most basic instincts."

Justine H., Seattle

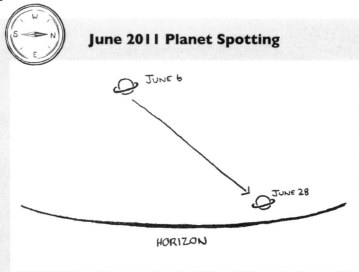

June 2011 Planet Spotting

Look west for Saturn from June 6 to 28.
The arrow indicates daily planet movement
throughout the month.

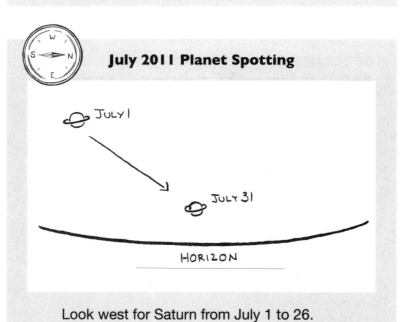

July 2011 Planet Spotting

Look west for Saturn from July 1 to 26.
The arrow indicates daily planet movement
throughout the month.

Astronomy

Just the Tip

Halley's Comet

If you want a surefire celestial sighting and you're extremely patient, Halley's Comet is scheduled to appear sometime in 2061. With any luck, we'll be able to control the weather by then, though, because if it's cloudy that day, you're going to be screwed for another 75 years.

August 2011 Planet Spotting

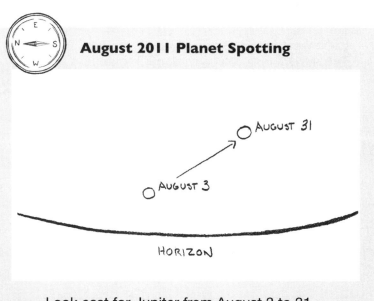

Look east for Jupiter from August 3 to 31. The arrow indicates daily planet movement throughout the month.

June 2012 Planet Spotting

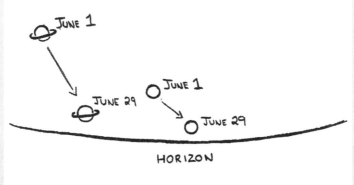

Look west for Saturn and Mars from June 1 to 29. The arrows indicate daily planet movement throughout the month.

July 2012 Planet Spotting

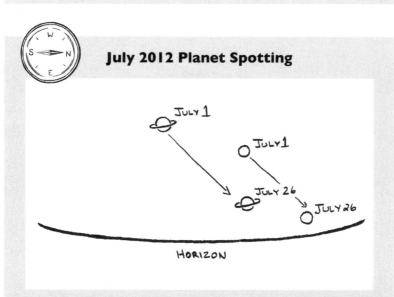

Look west for Saturn and Mars from July 2 to 26. The arrows indicate daily planet movement throughout the month.

Astronomy

August 2012 Planet Spotting

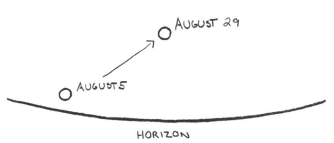

O August 29

O August 5

HORIZON

Look east for Jupiter from August 5 to 29. The arrow indicates daily planet movement throughout the month.

On Good Terms

The Milky Way: The Milky Way is a spiral galaxy consisting of more than 200 billion stars, including the pale yellow dot we call our sun. The galaxy is so named because it vaguely resembles a cloudy little splash of milk. Seeing the awe-inspiring band of light is one of the only times it is acceptable to cry over spilled milk (another is if it's the last of your milk and you were really craving Count Chocula).

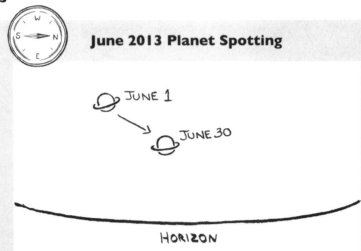

June 2013 Planet Spotting

JUNE 1

JUNE 30

HORIZON

Look west for Saturn from June 1 to 30.
The arrow indicates daily planet
movement throughout the month.

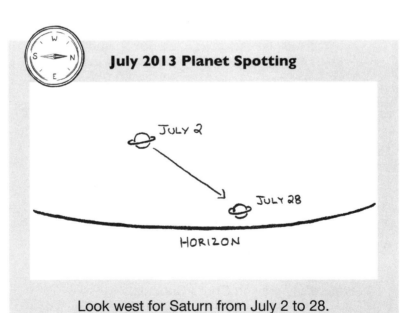

July 2013 Planet Spotting

JULY 2

JULY 28

HORIZON

Look west for Saturn from July 2 to 28.
The arrow indicates daily planet
movement throughout the month.

Astronomy

August 2013 Planet Spotting

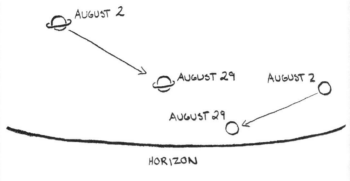

AUGUST 2

AUGUST 29

AUGUST 2

AUGUST 29

HORIZON

Look west for Saturn and Venus from August 2 to 29. The arrows indicate daily planet movement throughout the month.

Just the Tip

Unlike stars, planets don't twinkle. So to confirm that what you're looking at is a planet, stare long enough to twinkle-check. If everything still seems to twinkle, you might have acute glaucoma. In that case, get back inside and make an appointment to see an optometrist.

If all the stars in the visible cosmos are a massive ink blot, constellations would be the result of an insane ancient Rorschach test. Somehow, the Greeks managed to take six or seven random stars and use them to construct all sorts of arbitrary shapes—a dilapidated sea monster, a prancing centaur, a pair of creepily codependent twins.

With a little help from us and some imagination from you, it's still possible to see these ancient star formations as they were originally defined. We've raided our local planetarium and picked out three easy-to-spot summertime constellations. We also provide you with somewhat precise locations and semi-accurate backstories. All so that the next time you look up at the stars, you won't just be able to pick out misshapen mythological beasts— you'll be reminded of the time your date undid your Orion's Belt and took out her Gemini Twins.

On Good Terms

Summer Triangle: A section of the northern hemisphere's celestial sphere noted for its visibility during the summer months. All three constellations that we're going to discuss are located in the Summer Triangle.

Cygnus (sig-nuhs), The Swan

Myth: Seduction

Zeus became enamored with Leda, the queen of Sparta, probably because she was the only woman living at the time who he hadn't had sex with. Leda refused him, so Zeus transformed himself into a swan, because he was too much of an idiot to just turn a swan into a hot chick. Leda naively allowed this swan to rest on her lap, and once she fell asleep, Zeus had his way with her. If this all sounds a bit "rapey," that's only because there were different standards of morality back in the days of Greek mythology. If you were to dress up in a swan outfit and sneak into Buckingham Palace to sexually assault Queen Elizabeth II, it's not likely you'd be rewarded with your own constellation.

Star Search

Cygnus is easy to spot because its foremost stars form a recognizable cross. The brightest star in the constellation, Deneb, is located in the swan's stubby little tail. That bright star is one of the corners of the Summer Triangle.

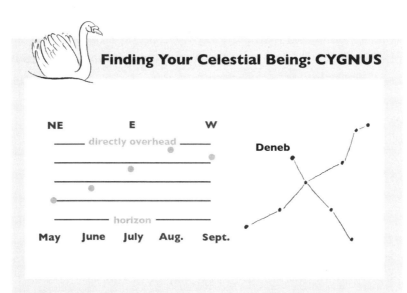

Finding Your Celestial Being: CYGNUS

NE   E   W

directly overhead

Deneb

horizon

May   June   July   Aug.   Sept.

Shown 11 p.m. DST on the 15th of every month. If viewing earlier/later, adjust one month for every two hours.

Example: If it's 9 p.m. in August, then refer to the June location.

Just the Tip

To locate each of the constellations, first start by
locating the North Star, then use the graphs to
pinpoint its exact location.

Aquila [uh-kwil-uh], The Eagle

Myth: Zeus's Personal Eagle

Aquila was Zeus's pet eagle. He was MAD Cat to Zeus's Dr. Claw,
Mini-Me to Zeus's Dr. Evil—a wingman with wings. Anytime somebody messed with Zeus, Aquila was there with thunderbolts in his
beak and a death stare smoldering in his beady little eyes. When
Prometheus stole fire on behalf of humankind, for example, Zeus
chained him naked to a mountain and sent Aquila to continuously
attack his flesh. Aquila pecked away at Prometheus for years,
never even pausing to inquire what the former Titan had done.
Aquila was the fearsome eagle enforcer to Zeus's one-man mafia.

Star Search

This constellation is conspicuous thanks to its bright star Altair,
which is the southern point of the Summer Triangle. Although
Altair is bright, the rest of Aquila is a lot dimmer, so a dark sky is
relatively important when tracing Aquila. And keep in mind that
while this constellation is easy to spot, it resembles an eagle
about as much as it resembles Super Mario.

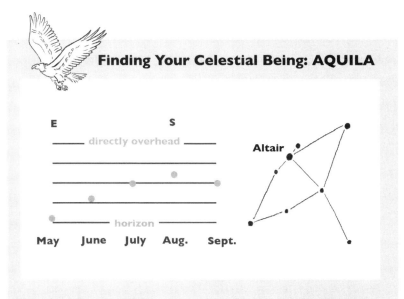

Finding Your Celestial Being: AQUILA

Shown 11 p.m. DST on the 15th of every month. If viewing earlier/later, adjust one month for every two hours.

Example: If it's 9 p.m. in August, then refer to the June location.

Lyra [lahy-ruh], The Stringed Instrument

Myth: The Gig From Hell

After his wife Eurydice died, Orpheus wasn't content to just throw her a funeral. The "father of songs" instead descended into the bowels of the underworld to bring her back, bringing with him his trademark lyre (which is similar to a small harp). Hades was either extremely impressed by Orpheus' music or was just irritated by the noise and wanted him to leave; either way, he agreed to release Eurydice. His only condition was that Orpheus couldn't glance back at his wife as the two of them ascended back to the world of the living, which of course Orpheus successfully managed to screw up. His wife turned to dust, and he was left playing sad emo music until his merciful death. This was the most tragic event in the music industry up until Susan Boyle.

Star Search

Considered the gem of the northern sky, Lyra is clearly defined by its brilliant star Vega. Vega is the northern corner of the Summer Triangle. If you listen closely on an especially quiet night, you can faintly hear Orpheus strumming impassioned 1980s power ballads.

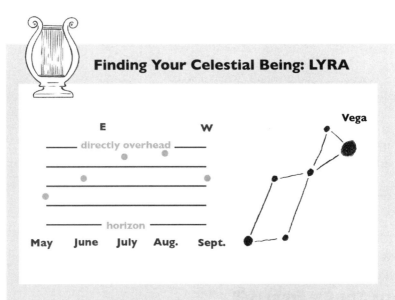

Finding Your Celestial Being: LYRA

Shown 11 p.m. DST on the 15th of every month. If viewing earlier/later, adjust one month for every two hours.

Example: If it's 9 p.m. in August then refer to the June location.

❝❞ Quintessential Quotation

"For small creatures such as we the vastness is bearable only through love."
—*Carl Sagan*, Astronomer

Astronomy

Just the Tip

Shooting stars aren't actually stars, but meteors—that is, conglomerations of rock and ice hurtling into Earth's atmosphere. It's unlikely you'll happen to see one, and that's a good thing. Shooting stars can't actually grant wishes, and if they're large enough, they could decimate civilization. Getting laid during the advent of nuclear winter is probably a tough sell.

A Sure Thing — Astrology 101

Let's get this out of the way: although it was once intertwined with astronomy, astrology has far more in common with palm readings and parlor tricks. Nevertheless, accruing a rudimentary understanding of mythical space beasts can have far more poignant and relevant implications to your life than you probably have realized. The benevolent gods have not only granted you a way to justify nearly every one of your aberrations, but have also supplied you with a steady stream of pickup lines.

For example, the next time you're arrested for urinating on your estranged neighbor's azaleas, you'll have a perfectly good excuse. If you are a Sagittarius, you could explain that you are a provider, often giving part of yourself to others and that you will reconnect with someone you have not seen in a long time. What's amazing is that this same prophecy can be used to seduce and explain your chance meeting with that hot girl from last semester's French Lit class. Knowing just a little astrology can go a long way toward helping you align your stars with a heavenly body back here on earth.

Aries (The Ram)
March 21 to April 19

Personality traits:
Adventurous, energetic, enthusiastic, confident

Compatible signs:
Leo and Sagittarius

Ruled by:
Mars

In relationships:
Aries are considered sexually pro-miscuous. Being the first sign in the zodiac, they also like to finish first, which in the case of men can be a real problem for their poor girlfriends.

Taurus (The Bull)
April 20 to May 20

Personality traits:
Patient, reliable, introverted, determined

Compatible signs:
Taurus and Virgo

Ruled by:
Venus

In relationships:
Sexually desiring but not sexually adventurous. These girls are like the namesake car: practical and trustworthy, but unlikely to offer any surprises. So they probably aren't look-ing to put any cargo in their trunks.

Gemini (The Twins)
May 21 to June 20

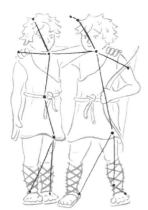

Personality traits:
Adaptable, versatile, communicative, witty

Compatible signs:
Libra and Aquarius

Ruled by:
Mercury

In relationships:
Sexually creative, but quickly interested in the next partner to come along. They're probably not relationship material, but lure two Geminis back to your place and you could be looking at a Gemini twin threesome.

Cancer (The Crab)
June 21 to July 22

Personality traits:
Emotional, intuitive, protective, sympathetic

Compatible signs:
Scorpio and Pisces

Ruled by:
Moon

In relationships:
Cancers are nurturers, and exceedingly loyal and loving in relationships. Just like the disease, your feelings for them will spread throughout your body, slowly overtaking you from the inside and eventually claiming your heart.

Astronomy

Leo (The Lion)
July 23 to August 22

Personality traits:
Generous, warmhearted, broad-minded, expansive

Compatible signs:
Aries and Sagittarius

Ruled by:
Sun

In relationships:
Leos have limitless sexual appetites and are willing to go all out to show you their affection. On the other hand, they're high-maintenance: They want expensive restaurants, tons of flowers, and enough oral to require the purchase of a snorkeler's mask.

Virgo (The Virgin)
August 23 to September 22

Personality traits:
Meticulous, reliable, practical, analytical

Compatible signs:
Taurus and Capricorn

Ruled by:
Mercury

In relationships:
For Virgos, sex is about a perfection of technique more than the expression of passion, so they should definitely know what they're doing. Pretty ironic when you consider that their sign is the Virgin.

Libra (The Scales)
September 23 to October 22

Scorpio (The Scorpion)
October 23 to November 21

Personality traits:
Easygoing, charming, idealistic, sociable

Compatible signs:
Gemini and Aquarius

Ruled by:
Venus

In relationships:
Romantic to the point of cheesiness, Libras enjoy pleasing their partners but prefer to keep things classy. That means the "pearl necklace" you give her should contain actual pearls.

Personality traits:
Determined, forceful, emotional, intuitive

Compatible signs:
Cancer and Pisces

Ruled by:
Pluto

In relationships:
Complicated in relationships, but the most passionate and sexually energetic of all the signs. Scorpios seek powerful sexual relationships, characterized by passionate displays of affection and light-to-moderate hair pulling.

Sagittarius
(The Archer/Centaur)
November 22 to
December 21

Personality traits:
Honest, straightforward, jovial, good-humored

Compatible signs:
Aries and Leo

Ruled by:
Jupiter

In relationships:
They are considered sexually controlled, and prefer to establish a firm spiritual connection. They're also the type of people who would actually use the phrase "firm spiritual connection."

Capricorn
(The Sea-Goat)
December 22 to
January 19

Personality traits:
Practical, prudent, ambitious, disciplined

Compatible signs:
Taurus and Virgo

Ruled by:
Saturn

In relationships:
Faithful to the point of jealousy, Capricorns are ambitious in the bedroom but will check your text-messaging history while you're taking a shower. Keep your Facebook password secure and a restraining order at the ready.

Aquarius
(The Water Carrier)
January 20 to
February 19

Personality traits:
Friendly, humanitarian, independent, intellectual

Compatible signs:
Gemini and Libra

Ruled by:
Uranus

In relationships:
Faithful in relationships and said to possess strong powers of attraction, Aquariuses are also open to experimentation. So it's probably fitting that they're ruled by Uranus.

Pisces
(The Two Fish)
February 20 to
March 20

Personality traits:
Imaginative, sensitive, compassionate, kind

Compatible signs:
Cancer and Scorpio

Ruled by:
Neptune

In relationships:
Pisces are intensely faithful and giving in relationships, and love being plied with gifts. This will come in handy if you ever make the mistake of implying that you find another woman attractive, because Pisces are also extremely sensitive.

Astronomy

Of course, there's a chance your date is too pragmatic to buy into astrology. Really, this is win/win, because it's all the more likely she'll be bowled over by your newfound astronomical knowledge. Apply what you've learned and you'll no longer have to rely on the planets aligning to pick up women.

Astronomy

French

Not Quite Enough — Pardon Your French Accent

Almost Enough — The French You Already Know

Just Enough — Les *Trois* A's of Acting French

A Sure Thing — Sealing It with a French Kiss

*M*ost guides about the subject of French delve into such trivialities as how to speak and understand the language. Why bother with that senseless masochism? You're trying to get laid, not become—pardon our French—a fucking diplomat. There's a lot we can learn from the French, and fortunately we don't need to rewire the language center of our brains to make use of it.

Let's examine for a moment the stereotypical French guy. He exhibits all the traits women find irresistible. Cutting-edge fashion? Yes. Emotional sensitivity? Yes. Is he a pretentious asshole? *Oui*. If someone set out with the sole purpose of creating an entire culture based simply on scoring chicks, they couldn't do a better job than the French have managed to pull out of their derrieres. Not convinced? Take a look at French President Nicolas Sarkozy's wife, Carla Bruni. She's treasonously hot. The best America ever did was Jackie O. If her eyes were any farther apart she would have been able to look around the corner of the book depository and spot the second shooter.

The allure women feel toward anything French starts young. Peek inside a typical French language class and you'll see what we're talking about. It'll be stocked top to bottom with girls desperate to surround themselves with this cultural representation of their romantic fantasy. Women fall for the French way

French

of life, not just the language. It's the attitude that's appealing. By embracing your own inner Frenchiness, you'll tap into a softer machismo—one that wields greater power than a typical brute-force approach.

Consider for a moment the reception you might receive for pro-posing to your date that she make out with her friend while having sex with you. Under typical circumstances this gesture would be met with less than enthusiasm, possibly resulting in testicular injury. That same request made with the panache of a Frenchman might have a decidedly different result. So next time propose instead an elegant ménage à trois. Never before has anything sounded so dignified and classy.

The ability to discreetly demonstrate all the traditionally French traits—aloofness, relaxed charm, style—will allow you to go through women like Grey Poupon at a Rolls Royce convention. Because even those of us who can't find Europe on a map know that French is the language of love. And that's not just because it sounds romantic; if you use it correctly, it can lead to a genuine French connection in the bedroom. The next few pages will teach you enough about French to score, but not enough that you'll surrender during wartime.

 The Bare Necessities

Appreciation for the arts, cultivated fashion sense, condescending attitude, $2,000 titanium bicycle (with basket), access to fresh baguettes, mustache comb.

Not Quite Enough — Pardon Your French Accent

Learning the entire French language sounds pretty gratuitous once you realize that the accent alone offers most of the same benefits. The quickest way into a woman's pants can be through her ears. And the soft, lulling intonations of the French accent provide a musical quality that's easy to associate with intimacy. It's also useful for when you're trying to convince student-loan collectors that you've relocated. It doesn't matter if you're describing how you make a living embezzling money from children's hospitals; as long as your voice is being filtered through the honeyed cadence of a Francophone, any girl within earshot will still consider sleeping with you—and possibly even help track down some vulnerable children's hospitals.

I. The French "R"

The most important element of the French accent (and the trickiest) is pronouncing your R's with a sort of guttural, gargling "h" sound. There is nothing equivalent in the English language, so this may be a new sound for you unless you've ever been close to drowning.

Begin by pushing the back of your tongue against the top of your mouth. Keep the tip of your tongue relaxed.

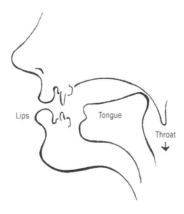

Now pretend like you're coughing up a pubic hair. The air should come up from the back of your throat and hit the back of your tongue. While making this hacking noise, produce an "h" sound. Your lips should look something like this:

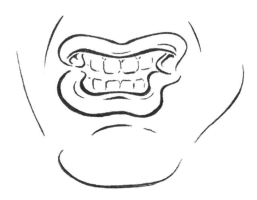

Practice on the word "raunchy." Done properly it should sound more like "rghaunchy." Try to minimize the spitting while maximizing the snootiness.

2. Replace "Th" with "Dz"

Soft "th" sounds—as in "there," "this" and "though"—should be replaced with a strong "dz." The "dz" is pronounced by pressing the front of your tongue against the back of your front teeth. Practice by saying the sentence, "This is not a purse; this is my satchel": "Dzis is not a purse; dzis is my satchel."

3. Replace Short "I" Sounds with "Ee"

Short "i" sounds, such as in "dish" and "sit," are pronounced more like "ee," as in "pee." Practice saying "prick" as the softer, friendlier-sounding *preek*.

4. Keep Your "H" Silent

Words such as "hungry" and "hippo" should be pronounced by dropping the "h" sound entirely, making the words "ungry" and "ippo." Instead of saying "handjob," practice asking for a "andjob."

5. Stress the Last Syllable

Unlike in English where the second-to-last syllable of a word is often stressed (com-PUT-er), the French almost always stress the last syllable (com-put-ER). This is the element of the accent that really gives it that sing-song quality. Don't say, "What a DOUCHEbag"; practice saying the much more melodic, "What a doucheBAG."

Almost Enough —The French You Already Know

By virtue of knowing English, you already know a fair amount of French. We've assembled a short list of some classic French loan words to get you in the right frame of mind. You'll often hear unimaginative simpletons drop them into their daily conversation to compensate for their overwhelming lack of verbal sophistication— and the thing is, it works. With these words you can come off like a frog-leg-eating, beret-wearing, existentialist-philosophy-reading snob without ever cracking the spine of your English-to-French dictionary.

Blasé (blah-**zey**): unimpressed with something because of over-familiarity.

> Example: Ever since the internet came along, I've felt so blasé about conventional pornography.

Bourgeois (boor-**zhwah**): derogatory term applying to people whose beliefs, attitudes and practices are conventionally middle-class.

> Example: Finding a parking spot at Whole Foods is impossible because of all the bourgeois twats who shop there.

C'est la vie (say la **vee**): "That's life."

> Example: I've been permanently banned from entering yet another Walgreens. C'est la vie.

Chic (sheek): stylish.

> Example: I can't tell if that dude is a shabby-chic hipster or a homeless lumberjack.

Coup de grâce (kood^uh **grahs**): literally, "blow of mercy"; the final blow that results in victory.

> Example: When it's been months since my girlfriend has gone down on me, my signature coup de grâce is to ask for a mercy blow.

French

Haute couture (oht koo-**too** r)**:** literally, "high sewing"; trend-setting fashion.

> Example: Everybody thought the fashion model had discovered the latest in haute couture, but she'd actually just gotten stuck in a birdcage.

Je ne sais quoi (zhuh n^{uh} se **kwa**)**:** literally, "I don't know"; an indefinable, elusive quality.

> Example: The aroma of one's own flatulence has a certain je ne sais quoi.

Raconteur (rak-uh n-**tur**)**:** a skilled storyteller.

> Example: My cousin Burt became a real raconteur once he fell off the wagon.

Just Enough — Les *Trois* A's of Acting French

To get laid like the French, one must act like the French. It's not just a matter of throwing on a beret, smoking unfiltered cigarettes and denigrating Americans—we've taken the liberty of figuring all this out for you by distilling the key cultural characteristics into three all-encompassing A's: Attitude, Appearance and Being Articulate. Follow our guide closely or you might fuck something up and inadvertently end up acting French Canadian, which won't help get you laid at all. In fact, it might cause others to think you have a learning disability.

Attitude (*maniére*)

It's tempting to besmirch the French based on all their stereotypical personality traits. If you go by reputation alone, the French have the work ethic, aloofness and skittishness of a common household cat. But examine these traits closely and you'll see they're actually the driving force behind women's obsession with French men. So you'd do well to stop mocking the French and start pillaging their personalities to get laid. And then you can go back to mocking them.

I. Putting Pleasure First

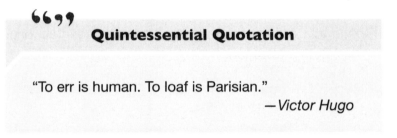

Quintessential Quotation

"To err is human. To loaf is Parisian."

— *Victor Hugo*

The French are often pigeonholed as lazy, but they're really just passionate about not working. Threaten to raise the legal age of retirement by three and a half days, and they'll take to the streets and begin maniacally settingas personal life; marathon two-hour lunch breaks mean a husband can catch a midday meal with his wife, with enough time left over to grab a quick bite with his mistress. The French understand that when you bring your work home with you, it means you're also bringing it home to your significant other. And it's impossible to make love with any energy when your head is still stuck in a cubicle.

2. Paragons of Arrogance

French waiters have probably earned their reputation for snooti-ness. Try complaining to one that you were served the wrong wine, and he'll react as though he'd personally invited you into his home for dinner and you responded by shitting upon his dining room table. In France the customer is always an idiot, especially if he's an American. This attitude, it's safe to say, extends well outside the confines of the service industry. But that which we interpret as arrogance, women respond to as confidence, which is the most potent pheromone known to man. You don't always have to know what you're talking about—you just have to act like it.

3. Lovers, Not Fighters

Using recent military history as a guide, it seems unlikely that you could challenge a Frenchman to a game of Scrabble without him forfeiting after five minutes. This is a bit of a caricature, but the equation of Frenchiness with docility is pretty widespread—as is, of course, its association with romantic idealism. For women this is win-win; all the masculine aggression is filtered into the efforts of producing art, cooking food and indulging in sublime sensuality. Pacifism doesn't just save lives. It gets lives laid.

French

 View from a Broad

"French guys look straight into your eyes when they are talking to you. Ok. Sometimes their eyes stray away towards your boobs, but quickly they come back to meet your eyes."

Princessa, New York, NY

French Lesson (*Leçon de Français*)

If your attitude is a success, chances are your date will comment on it. Let's complete your Frenchification by arming you with an appropriate French-language response to really knock her sacre bleus off.

For example, suppose she says something like: "You're different from the other guys I know." Depending on whether she's referring to your pleasure-first mentality, your arrogance or your nonaggressive disposition, here are some replies you can throw at her:

English: Thank you. Let's call in sick to work tomorrow and spend the whole day in bed.

French: Merci, prenons un jour de maladie demain et restons au lit toute la journée.

English: I'm not really being arrogant if I truly am the greatest man in history.

French: Je ne suis pas complètement arrogant si je suis vraiment le plus grand homme de l'histoire du monde.

English: Fighting is for children. I'm a man.

French: Les disputes sont pour les enfants, je suis un homme.

French

Appearance (*apparence*)

The French are big believers in the clothes-make-the-man mentality, which can be somewhat off-putting for those of us who primarily wear sweatpants and whatever we caught from the stadium T-shirt cannon—or at best shop at Men's Wearhouse, as if there were some prestige associated with shopping in a place named after a fucking storage facility. Between this, Burlington Coat Factory and the Dress Barn, American clothing retailers have somehow gotten it in their heads that we desperately want to be shopping in industrial buildings fit for cattle.

The French, meanwhile, prefer not to view their clothing as the end result of an impersonal industrial process, but as the product of a tailor's artful hand. One might derisively call the French "metrosexual," but it's hard to justifiably criticize a person for taking care in his appearance. And you can go ahead and mock them; they'll be laughing all the way to the Bank of Fellatio. Using the French as our inspiration, we've thrown together a few simple steps to looking good.

French

Wear clothing that fits

Most guys wear clothes that are too big. The French have figured out that they look their best when their clothes fit snugly, but aren't so tight that somebody could deduce whether they dress to the left or right. You don't need to spring for a tailor-fitted wardrobe, but because all clothing brands have a different fit, stopping off at the fitting room before you break out your credit card is absolutely essential. Here's how to find the perfect fit:

Shirt (*chemise*)

There are five areas of a shirt to consider: the neck, chest, back, cuffs and waist. These elements must combine their powers in the same way Captain Planet was summoned only when all the Planeteers worked as a team—even that useless shithead who had the power of "heart." But instead of fighting pollution, your shirt's only job is to sculpt a masculine shape out of the series of lumps constituting your upper body.

1. Collar (*col*): An overly tight collar will make you feel perpetually strangled, while anything too loose will cause you to appear oddly out of proportion. A good rule of thumb is that if you can work in about two fingers between your neck and the collar, your shirt is fit to be entered. If you can fist the area, however, you'll probably want to dial back a size.

2. Chest (*poitrine*): The key word here is "snug", not "tight". The outline of the long-expired condom you keep in your breast pocket shouldn't be visible.

3. Back (*dos*): The seam of the shirt should lie flat against your upper back and slope evenly downward. Shirts that are a size too large can puff out in the back.

4. Cuff (*poignet*): Your shirt cuffs should neither creep halfway down your hands, nor stop midway down your arms as if they were a baseball tee. You'll want the cuffs to fully cover your wrists and extend to the very base of your thumbs.

French

5. Waist (*taille*): Ideally, you'll have just enough room at the waist to give your beer gut some breathing room, even while seated. The buttons are designed to keep your shirt together, not act as a levee for your belly fat.

Quintessential Quotation

"Going to war without France is like going deer hunting without your accordion."
—*Norman Schwartzkopf*

Tie (*cravate*)

Nothing looks nice when it's clipped on—not nails and certainly not neckties. They scream "Mommy wasn't here to dress me" and are best left for mall security.

The Four-in-Hand Knot (*le nœud de cravate*)

The only time your collar should be popped is for the length of time it takes for you to put on a tie—which should only take a few seconds with the four-in-hand. You don't need to have received a Boy Scout merit badge in knot-tying to figure this one out. It's as easy as tying your shoe, and you don't even have to bend over.

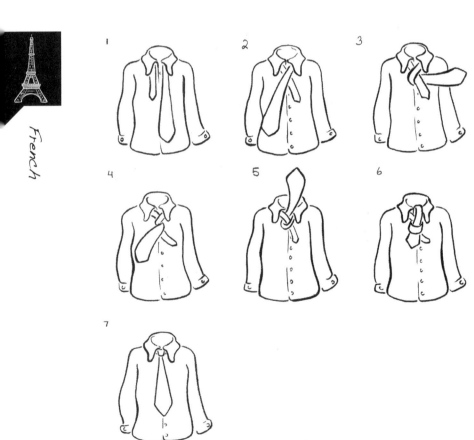

Pants (*pantalon*)

Pants are easy. There're really only two things you have to worry about when finding the right pants: figuring out your waist size and figuring out your length. Somehow, however, this proves a challenge for people, whose pants either sag down past the pelvis or are tight enough to constrict blood flow. Here's how to find the perfect pants:

I. Waist (*taille*): Your pants should come up to just be-low your navel, around where your ass crack tapers off—think somewhere in between Steve Urkle and Kriss Kross. They should feel snug enough to stay up without a belt, but not so tight that they leave an imprint.

2. Length (*longueur*): The break, or bottom of your pants should touch your shoe but not drape over it. If you're sit-ting with one leg propped up on your opposite knee, your pants should be in position to spare the world from seeing your hairy ankles.

French Lesson (*Leçon de Français*)

If she says, "Wow, you really know how to dress," here's how to respond:

English: Man is naked without fashion.

French: L'homme est nu, sans la mode.

English: The two most vital senses for a man is his common sense and his sense of style.

French: Les deux sens vitaux pour un homme sont: son bon sens et son sens vestimentaire.

English: Take your time getting dressed. It makes it easier finding someone who wants to undress you quickly.

French: Prenez votre temps pour bien vous habiller, ce sera plus facile de trouver quelqu'un qui vous déshabillera rapidement.

English: My looks will fade. My style will live forever.

French: Mon apparence se fanera, mon style sera eternel.

English: I put my pants on just like the you—one leg at a time. Then somehow I also manage to squeeze in my huge package.

French: J'enfile mon pantalon comme tout le monde—une jambe après l'autre. Puis, je me débrouille pour y introduire mes gros joyaux.

French

Just the Tip

French filmmakers are no strangers to romantic themes, though it's not like they have much of a choice. By virtue of location and language alone, pretty much any film set in France is going to be at least a little romantic. A French murder mystery would probably make a better date movie than some shitty Kate Hudson rom-com, but when the French film is actually intended to be romantic? You're talking instant Blu-ray BJ. With that in mind, here's a list of some ideal French films for watching with a girl.

- *A Man and a Woman*
  (Un homme et une femme), 1966
- *Cyrano de Bergerac*, 1990
- *The Taste of Others*
  (Le Goût des autres), 2000
- *Amélie*
  (Le Fabuleux destin d'Amélie Poulain), 2001
- *A Very Long Engagement*
  (Un long dimanche de fiançailles), 2004
- *The Diving Bell and the Butterfly*
  (Le scaphandre et le papillon), 2007

French

Being Articulate (*bien s'exprimer*)

The French revere their language almost as much as they revere themselves, which is pretty impressive. They actually go so far as to set firm legal limits on the introduction of new words, banning contemporary English lingo like "email" and "blog." Their goal is to keep the language chaste by avoiding the penetration of American terminology into their virginal lexicon. God forbid something upset the perfect poetic equilibrium of the French tongue.

On Good Terms

The Toubon Law regulates and protects the use of the French language in official French government publications.

This is all an unabashed manifestation of French arrogance, to be sure. But when you consider the cruelty with which Americans treat the English language, it starts to make a lot of sense. If there's any reason for looking up to the French, it's in their appreciation for language. And while it may seem counterintuitive to learn English grammatical rules in a chapter about French, you'd be surprised how important this is to girls. Here are some common abuses of the English language that should be avoided at all costs:

- **"Irregardless"** is not a word. Actually, it's technically listed in most dictionaries as a nonstandard word, but it'll still make you sound like an idiot. **"Regardless"** is what you're trying to say.

- Avoid saying **"could of"** or **"should of."** The correct syntax is **"should have"** and **"would have."**

- **"Fewer"** and **"less"** are not interchangeable. **"Fewer"** refers to countable nouns—as in, "I have fewer than three friends." **"Less"** refers to uncountable nouns—things like debt, rain, sadness, etc.—as in, "There has been less rain ever since the rain dancing union went on strike."

- Saying **"Me and Paul went to Blockbuster"** doesn't make sense, and not just because nobody rents movies from Blockbuster anymore. Think about it this way: If you were to remove Paul from the sentence, you'd be left with, "Me went to Blockbuster," which makes you sound like a Neanderthal. The original sentence should be, "**Paul and I went to Blockbuster**, but then decided to sign up for Netflix."

When corresponding with a girl via SMS, email or Craigslist casual encounters, it's also important to avoid basic written mistakes, the most common of which involve homonyms and contractions. These may sound like harmless errors, but it will provoke miniature brain aneurysms in any girl who's sensitive to this sort of thing.

> **Your/You're:** "Your" is used to indicate possession ("Could I sleep with your sister?"). "You're" is a contraction of "you are."

> **Its/It's:** "Its" indicates possession ("Success is its own reward"). "It's" is a contraction of "it is."

> **Their/They're/There:** "Their" indicates possession. "They're" is a contraction of "they are." "There" is usually used as an adverb and usually relates to location.

> **Too/To:** Use "too" when meaning "excessively" or "also," as in, "There are too many people in my bathtub" or "I'm aroused, too." "To" can safely be used everywhere else.

> **Then/Than:** "Then" relates to time. "Than" is used to make comparative statements. "He got more Asian women than I did back then."

A Sure Thing — Sealing It with a French Kiss

The term "French kiss" dates back to at least the 1920s, though the French hardly invented it. That we refer to it as a French kiss reveals less about its country of origin than it does about our own association of Gallic culture with sexual proclivity. You could use the word "French" with any otherwise innocent activity and as a prefix to it would somehow just sound more titillating: "French tickle," "French oil change," "French bank withdrawal." Use "German" as a prefix for these same words and they just sound ominous and potentially painful.

VideoMark:
How to French Kiss

Whatever its origins, French kiss refers to passionate tongue kissing. Much like poker, comedy and photography, it's one of those things pretty much everybody thinks they're great at—but you don't have to speak with more than a couple of women to hear a dozen horror stories. We've done exactly that, using this firsthand guidance to compile a painfully simple guide to French kissing like a champion.

1. Clean Your Mouth

You should treat French kissing like a dental appointment: Brush and floss the shit out of your teeth beforehand. Create the illusion that your mouth is always clean. If nothing else, swig a bit of mouthwash. You don't want your date to be able to figure out what you had for dinner.

French

2. Close Your Eyes

There is a time and place for firm eye contact. Being a few inches from another person's face is not one of them. The only thing creepier than locking eyes during a French kiss would be to begin nonchalantly stroking your member.

3. Don't Give Her Mouth-to-Mouth Resuscitation

The trick is to build a little anticipation. Take your time. Begin with a closed-mouth kiss. Start gently and gradually build to a more passionate open-mouthed affair, but never to the point where you're eating her face.

4. A Little Tongue

The tongue should only be introduced after an appropriate buildup of lip kisses. At first, just brush her lips with your tongue. Don't immediately jam your tongue down her throat as if it were a SWAT team breaking down the door to a meth lab. Be playful, not aggressive—and remember that gentle is key.

French

5. Mutual Exploration

Feel free to do a little oral exploration with your tongue, but try not to completely mop up the inside of her mouth. Occasionally pull back. The goal here is reciprocation. Allow your partner to do a little exploration of her own.

6. Hands On

Your hands aren't meant to dangle awkwardly at your side. Cup her cheek at first, allowing you to draw her closer, and then position your hand at the back of her neck. If she's attempting to pull away, of course, you can go ahead and skip this step; some girls find too much hand contact to be a little invasive. If she's into it, however, you should have plenty of opportunity to let your hand stray elsewhere. At some point the boundaries between French kissing and other forms of physical intimacy begin to blur. And it's a good thing you never bothered learning the entire French language. If you've done everything right, there won't be much more need for talking.

French

Construction

196

*I*f there's one thing we've all learned from watching porn, it's that women will throw themselves at any plumber, electrician or carpenter who knocks on their door. All these guys have to do is show up in an old T-shirt and dirty jeans, carrying a toolbox, and every one of these hot, lonely women will be grabbing for his wing-nuts.

You don't see this kind of thing happening to lawyers or bankers. Women seem to be more attracted to the guy who builds the bookshelf than to the guy who reads the books. Put another way, women are drawn to guys who know how to use their tools. So what's the lesson here? For one thing, getting a degree from Harvard is a total waste of time when apparently all you need is a certificate from ITT Tech.

Construction

We realize that, for most of you, the only tools in your toolbox are an Allen wrench and a few "spare parts" left over from wrestling with your IKEA coffee table. That's okay. We're going to teach you just the basics, those day-to-day skills your father should have taught you: the proper way to use a drill, hammer a nail, find a stud and build a massage table.

So the next time she calls upon you to hang a picture, paint a wall or fix a sink, you'll know enough to grab your tool box, knock on her door and say, "Did somebody call for a plumber?"

The Bare Necessities

- Hammer
- Screwdrivers (Phillips, flat-head, Smirnoff/OJ)
- Pliers
- Tape measure (around 15′)
- Crescent wrench
- Utility knife
- Pencil
- Safety glasses
- Five o'clock shadow
- 3″ to 4″ plumber's crack

Construction

Not Quite Enough — Using Basic Tools

The ability to use complex tools is what separates us from lesser animals, like dolphins and children. But from a girl's perspective, it also tends to separate guys who can physically handle themselves from guys who wouldn't know what to do with a woman's body if they had a detailed blueprint and a team of laborers.

Getting Hammered

Pete Seeger once speculated that if he had a hammer, he'd hammer in the morning and evening, as well as all over this land. Thankfully for everyone in earshot, he never managed to acquire that hammer. If you've had better luck finding a hammer, let's quickly review the finer points of hitting a nail:

1. Hold your hammer about midway up the handle. Grab a nail and pinch it near the nail head, between your forefinger and thumb. Lightly tap from a distance of about 6 inches until it's standing upright on its own. You can also set the nail in the bristles of a comb while keeping a spare in the bristles of your mustache.

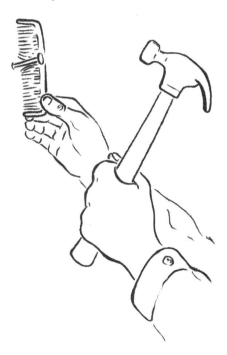

2. When you're ready to start swinging, use your whole arm and not just your wrist. Choke down on the hammer until your hand is about 2 inches away from the base, allowing you to generate ample force.

Construction

Driving a nail straight into the wall usually works fine, but driving it in at a slight angle can increase its holding power.

For Good Measure

Measuring is the most important aspect of any building project. Any mistake made in this stage will have lasting effects—hence the aphorism, "Measure twice, cut once." In other words, your tape measure has more important uses than merely measuring the length of your genitals. Besides, a simple water displacement test will yield more complete genital calculations.

A standard tape measure indicates both inches (at top) and centimeters (at bottom). The inches are typically divided into sixteenths, with other hash marks indicating ⅛, ¼ and ½ inches.

Construction

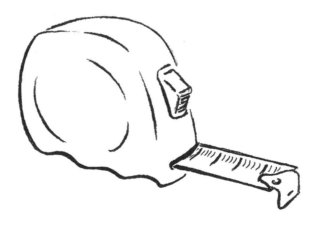

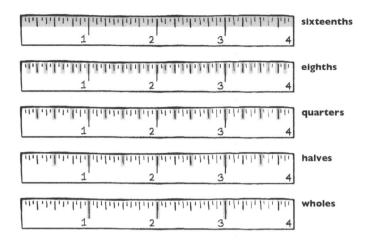

sixteenths

eighths

quarters

halves

wholes

Here's a visual reference.

This baby carrot is a laughable $1^3/_{16}$ inches.

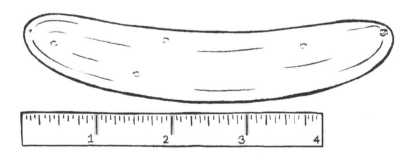

This cucumber is off the charts, with an imposing girth and naturally formed pleasure ridges.

Construction

Blue Balls Beware

Unspooling the entire length of your tape measure and then releasing the lock so that all the tape whips back into the case at high speed is a dangerous and childish pastime. Limit yourself to two or three episodes.

On the Level

Along with megaphones, levels are one of the only implements Ty Pennington's producers trust him to use on camera. If you're capable of recognizing what a bubble looks like, you can use a level.

1. Determine whether you need a 2-foot or 4-foot level. The 2-foot level is used for hanging photographs, artwork, mirrors, counterfeit medical degrees, etc. The 4-foot level is used for carpentry and is more accurate.

2. Whether leveling something horizontal or vertical, the same rules apply. Place the level on the surface of whatever you're trying to keep straight. If the bubble falls between the two etched lines, then you're good to go. If it doesn't, adjust accordingly until the bubble is in the sweet spot.

Famous Carpenters

Harrison Ford, Adam Carolla, Mike Holmes, Jesus, Bob Vila, Bob the Builder, ⅙ of the Village People, Charisma Carpenter, Jimmy Carter, The Carpenters

Almost Enough — All About Walls

The wall is a canvas on which the handyman demonstrates his mastery over the domicile—finding studs, tearing down ratty, coffee-stained wallpaper, and plugging all those mysterious holes. Being equipped to handle these tasks will make you extremely valuable to women.

It might be controversial to say, but we'd posit that a woman's real-life walls are even more important than her Facebook wall. Helping take care of them can lead to some real-life pokes.

Finding Studs

Studs are generally placed every 16 inches apart, so once you've found your first one, tracking down the next usually just requires a little measuring. And while you could dip into your swear jar fund for one of those pricey magnetic stud finders, the most elegant (and most impressive) way to find one is also the cheapest.

Construction

The Good, the Bad and the Studly:

1. Using the handle of your hammer, gently tap the wall along a horizontal line. Carefully listen to the sound this produces. It will sound heavier and more solid when you've located a stud.

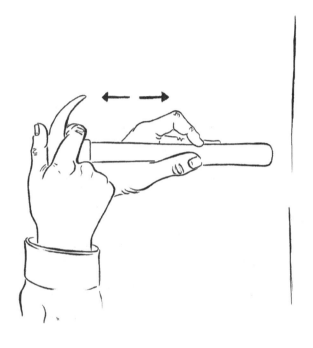

Just the Tip

Every 16 inches on your tape measure, there should be an arrow indicator. This is handy to note because 16 inches is the typical distance between the centers of two adjacent wall studs.

The Good, the Bad and the Studlier:

An even more accurate way to find a stud is by using a tape measure. This way, not only will you show her that you're tape-measure literate, you'll also demonstrate a seemingly superhuman x-ray mastery over the interior of your walls.

I. Start by locating a wall outlet or light switch, because it's usually directly attached to a stud (on either the left or right side).

Just the Tip

If there are no outlets or light switches where you're looking, start with a corner. Instead of measuring 16″ away to find your stud as you would normally do, adjust your measurement to 14¾″ from the corner (accounting for the thickness of the drywall).

2. Once you've marked the center of your first stud, remember that the next one will be 16″ away from the center.

Quintessential Quotation

"Every nail driven should be as another rivet in the machine of the universe."

— *Thoureau*

Removing Wallpaper

Whether it's a 1970s paisley print in your masturbatorium or an offensively tacky vegetable motif in your date's kitchen, wallpaper seems to age like dog years, becoming dated within moments of installation. You probably didn't put it up, but it's your responsibility to tear it down. And unlike removing your date's clothes, the results will almost always be satisfying.

1. Keeping your floor dry requires preparation. First tape plastic floor covering to your baseboards, allowing it to overlap the floor by about 2 feet. Press firmly on the tape to create a watertight seal. Cover the draped plastic with additional plastic, top that with towels, and then top that with a layer of your moisture-starved Chia pets.

On Good Terms

Wallpaper facing: The layer of wallpaper that has the design (or lack thereof).

Wallpaper backing: The second layer of wallpaper, which is where the adhesive that sticks to your walls is located.

Construction

2. Using a putty knife, start at the top of the wall and begin loosening the wallpaper facing. When you have a good, graspable corner, pull downward with your hands, applying steady pressure. You will have two layers to contend with, the facing and the backing. They will not come off in one satisfyingly even sheet no matter how hard you try.

3. Mix hot water together with fabric softener or vinegar (not both) at a 1:1 ratio. Use a sponge to scrub this mixture onto the remaining facing and backing. Let the wall absorb it for about 15 minutes. Depending on which mixture you made, you can use any leftovers to make the world's shittiest salad.

4. It's time to start scraping. Using an old spatula or dull putty knife, scrape the backing off the damp wall.

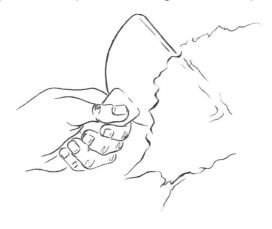

5. Once you've successfully detached all the paper from the wall, you'll need to remove the glue residue. Alternate between attacking it with your spatula or putty knife, and scrubbing at it with your sponge. Do this until absolutely all the glue has been removed, because if there's any left, it will either cause your wallpaper to bubble or your new paint to crack.

Filling Her Holes

The Bare Necessities

- Self-adhesive 1″ to 3″ mesh tape
- Utility knife
- Putty knife
- Fast-drying putty

There are limitless conceivable activities that can lead to unsightly drywall holes, and while most of those activities involve some form of alcohol, they all result in the same problem: There is a goddamn hole in your wall. The strategy many of us might take would be to simply set fire to the house, collect the insurance money, and then buy a similar house with a fully intact wall. But there's actually an easier, less circuitous way to address the problem.

1. Clean around the infected area of your hole, trimming away any broken wallboard.

Construction

2. Use sandpaper to roughen the area around the hole (this sounds more painful than it is). This will allow your mesh patch tape to stick. Depending on how gaping the hole is, you might need several strips.

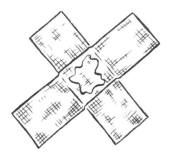

3. Using a putty knife, coat the hole with a layer of fast-drying all-purpose putty compound, lightly forcing it into the mesh. Smooth it out, leaving a layer just thick enough to cover the tape.

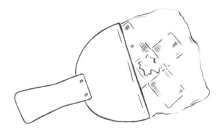

4. Apply two more coats of the compound in successively broader and thinner coats to blend the patch into the surrounding area.

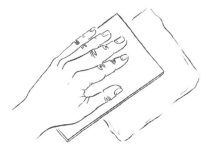

Construction

5. Allow your putty to dry, and find another hole to attend to. Be patient. If you don't wait for the putty to dry properly, it will crack and you'll find yourself starting over from scratch, having to stuff your date's hole a second time in the same evening. This can be physically draining.

6. After the putty dries, sand, prime and paint it to match the rest of the wall.

VideoMark:
Filling Her Holes

Just Enough —"Did Somebody Call for a Handyman?"

It's one thing to tool around with the basics, but to really impress a girl, you'll need to roll up your sleeves and delve into the most in-demand handyman skills: hanging up her priceless framed family photographs, painting her walls and recovering her jewelry from her sink. If your date lives in an apartment, she's probably sick of putting in maintenance requests with that mustachioed molester-landlord who always manages to show up just as she's stepping out of the shower. If she lives in a house, she probably calls upon her male BFF, which can also stand for "boning friends forever," to fix up her place. Take solace in knowing that the skills you are about to acquire will ensure that the only guy doing any screwing around her house will be you. You can discuss the fees for your services later.

Hanging a Picture

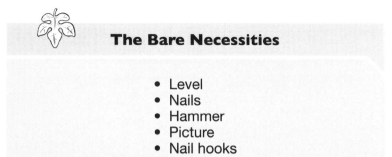

The Bare Necessities

- Level
- Nails
- Hammer
- Picture
- Nail hooks

The qualities you're looking to achieve when hanging a picture are the same qualities your date wants from you: it should be secure, straight and well-hung. A clumsy picture-hanging attempt can lead to a nightmarish scenario involving glass shards and a ruined visage of your date's grandmother, with you in the corner tangled up in picture wire.

I. Decide where you want the picture. Hold the frame up at eye level where the top meets the wall. Leave a pencil mark in the approximate center.

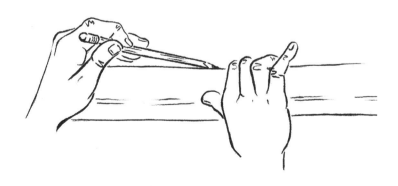

Construction

2. Bring down the picture and measure the distance from the top of the frame to the wire or hook in the back.

3. Using your measurement from Step 2 and the mark you left in Step 1, determine where the wire or hook will be positioned against the wall. Mark this spot with an "X" and hammer in a nail at a slight angle.

4. Hang the picture on the nail. Place a level on top of the picture and adjust it until it's straight.

VideoMark:
Hanging a Picture

Just the Tip

When mounting objects like a shelf or a heavier painting, you'll want to attach them to the studs you found in the wall. That's because neither drywall nor plaster walls will support much weight. If you do need to hang something substantial in a place where there's no stud, use a drywall anchor or a toggle bolt. Otherwise, your object is liable to come crashing down the next time a bus drives by, and you'll have yet another hole to patch.

Painting a Room

 The Bare Necessities

- Paint trays
- Sash brush (an angled brush used to edge around walls, ceilings, moldings and doors)
- Paint roller handles and covers
- Desired paint color
- Paint stirrers
- Stepladder (if painting an area out of reach)
- Drop cloths or old sheets (to keep couches and floors paint-free)
- Blue painter's tape

Before You Get Your Brush Wet

You've just spent two hours staring at color swatches to find the exact right shade of beige to complement your date's tacky furniture. Now the guy behind the paint counter has the audacity to ask, "What finish would you like?," as if you could even begin to understand what that means. Unfortunately, this isn't some secret Home Depot code for a post-paint-mixing happy ending. It's an important component for giving your walls the right sheen.

> **Flat finish:** This finish is good for large surfaces or wherever you don't want your paint reflecting light. It's recommended in bedrooms, living rooms, and dining rooms and on most ceilings—essentially, everywhere but kitchens and bathrooms. It's also the most common finish, so it's a pretty safe bet.

Gloss finish: Typically used in small quantities, this finish is designed to reflect light, especially on walls and ceilings. It's used a lot on trim.

Satin/eggshell finish: This finish is terrific for brightening up hallways, common areas. It can be used anywhere you want a slight sheen.

Semigloss finish: Used in high-traffic areas like kitchens and bathrooms, this finish is easy to keep clean. It's also popular on doors.

Just the Tip

A Primer on Primer
You'll want to first paint a layer of primer when painting on top of an older, grimier layer of paint.

Pre-Painting Preparations

1. Removing light-socket covers will make your life a whole lot easier when you paint. Just make sure you switch the power off before unscrewing anything.

2. Take a moment to quickly wash all visible dirt off your walls with soap and water. Paint won't stick as well to a dirty surface.

3. Move all of her furniture away from the walls and toward the center of the room. Once it's out of the way, cover it in old sheets to protect the furniture from paint splatters.

Putting an old washcloth or T-shirt under the corners of heavy furniture will allow you to move it effortlessly, making you appear to have superhuman strength.

4. Set down painter's tape along the moldings. Even with a steady hand, paint is bound to end up where it shouldn't.

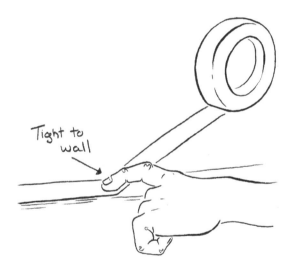

Tight to wall

Getting Some Trim...Painted

Painting a room is like foreplay: You'll want to start with the outside and work your way into the middle. In other words, first paint the perimeters of the walls, windows, doors, outlets and light switches before tackling the body of the wall itself.

Construction

1. Pop your paint can lid with a flat-head screwdriver and give the paint a good stir. There is actually technique to this. The idea here is to not just stir in circles, but to bring together the mixture from the bottom up. Work your wooden paint stirrer in an up-and-down circular motions.

2. Dip your sash brush into the paint, so about the third of the bristles are submerged. This is called "loading the brush"—one of the infinitely dirty-sounding phrases used in construction. The goal here is to get as much paint on the brush as possible without having paint run down the wall. Painters refer to this as "preventing the runs."

3. Using the narrow edge of the brush, paint along the edges of the room. Apply just enough force to flex your bristles and your arms. Paint with long, slow strokes.

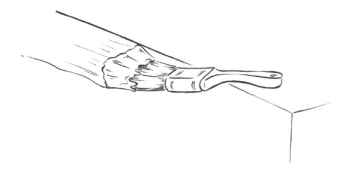

4. Move on to the corners, using the wide edge of the brush.

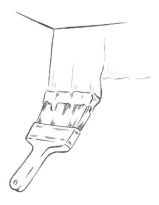

VideoMark:
Painting Trim

Painting the Walls

I. Once you've finished painting the perimeters of the wall, the rest is as easy as coloring within the lines. First, fill a roller pan about halfway full. Set the roller in the middle of the well and roll it a few times toward the top of the tray, along the ridges. Repeat this a few more times until your roller is evenly coated with paint but not so overloaded that it's dripping.

Construction

217

2. Start by painting a big "W," or paint the first letter of her name. Work in small 1 foot sections. Painting a "W" is ideal for preventing unwanted roller marks, but for a quick laugh you can also paint "red rum" all over the room.

Just the Tip

Begin your roller strokes in an upward direction. If you roll downward on your first stroke, the paint may puddle under the roller and drip down the walls.

3. Begin filling in the gaps with horizontal back–and-forth strokes.

4. Smooth the area out by lightly rolling vertically from the top to the bottom of the painted area. Lift the roller and return it to the top of the area after each stroke.

5. Wait for the paint to completely dry. You don't have to actually sit there and watch the paint dry. We're sure you and your date can think of something more exciting to do to kill the time.

Just the Tip

Always paint with a good lighting source, especially when applying the second coat. When painting a room for a girl, ideally you'll paint your first coat at night, forcing you to be there first thing in the morning to finish the job. And it'd probably be easiest to just wake up there. The natural early-morning light is great for revealing any imperfections in the paint surface.

VideoMark:
Painting the Walls

Retrieving Family Jewels from a Sink

Recovering jewelry from a sink drain is like having intercourse: the plumbing seems confusing at first, but with an adequate tool and a little elbow grease, the job can be done in no time at all. And of course, both activities also require a good clean rag and a plastic bucket. And if you do either successfully, she's bound to give you a call the next time her pipes need attention.

Construction

The Bare Necessities

- Channel Pliers
- A bucket
- A rag

219

1. Switch off the hot-and-cold water valves, which can be found under the sink.

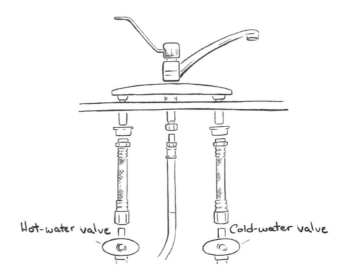

Hot-water valve   Cold-water valve

2. Test the faucet to confirm that the water is off.

3. Place your bucket beneath the sink.

4. Using channel pliers, loosen the slip nuts on the trap bend (the U-shaped portion of the pipe). Finish unscrewing them by hand.

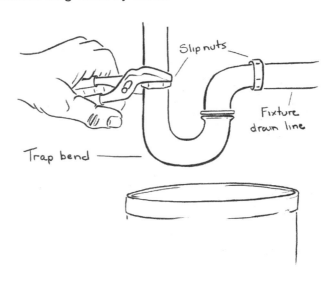

Slip nuts

Fixture drain line

Trap bend

5. Pull the trap bend down from the sink. The jewelry should have ended up in this part of the pipe, along with any hair, coins, pogs and other ancient crap that fell down the drain.

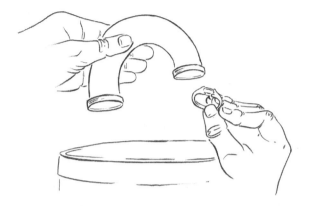

6. Reconnect the pipe and turn the valves back on.

VideoMark:
Retrieving Family
Jewels from a Sink

A Sure Thing — Building a Massage Table

You've made yourself helpful around the house, but you've still only scratched the plywood surface of what your little tools can do. We're going to teach you how to create the least practical, most extravagant handmade gift of all time: a massage table. If you somehow have problems getting laid after building this for a girl, you should be probably less concerned with learning construction than tracking down the gypsy who put a curse on your penis.

Construction

The Bare Necessities

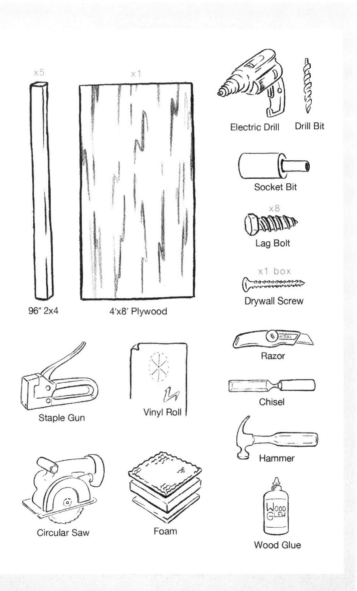

x5

x1

Electric Drill   Drill Bit

Socket Bit

x8

Lag Bolt

x1 box

Drywall Screw

96" 2x4   4'x8' Plywood

Razor

Chisel

Staple Gun   Vinyl Roll

Hammer

Circular Saw   Foam

Wood Glue

Using Your Tools

Circular saw: to trim down your 2x4s.

Jigsaw: to make the hole for her face in the plywood.

Power drill with a socket bit: to screw the lag bolts into the wood.

Staple gun: to attach your vinyl to the underside of the table.

Wood glue: to glue the padding onto the tabletop.

Knowing Your Wood

Five 8' 2x4s
One 4'x8' sheet of ¾" plywood

Using Your Hardware

Eight 3" lag bolts to attach the legs to the frame
One 3" box of drywall screws

Textiles Needed

One twin-bed foam mattress cover 2" to 3" thick 3 yards of vinyl to finish off your masterpiece. Because while you may want wood entering your date, you definitely don't want it to be in the form of splinters.

Preparing All the Pieces

The Easy Cuts

Here are all the cuts you need to make in order to assemble the pieces of the table.

Tools: circular saw

The legs: Using your 2x4s, cut four boards measuring 30″.

The short rails (head of the table): Using your 2x4s, cut two boards measuring 29″.

The long rails (sides of the table): Using your 2x4's, cut two boards measuring 68″.

The top: Cut your plywood to 36″x75″.

Construction

Just the Tip

If you don't have a circular saw, make friends with someone at Home Depot. They will cut the wood for you.

The Tough Cuts

Don't get nervous. The whole point of building a massage table is to relieve stress. Follow the directions and you should be just fine.

The Place for Her Face

Tools: jigsaw

In this cut, you're going to be making the hole in the plywood where she'll eventually be sticking her face.

1. Set the plywood on something sturdy and even, like a sawhorse or milk crates.

2. From one end of the plywood, measure down 12″. Make a mark. At that mark, draw a horizontal line across the plywood.

3. Find the center of the horizontal line. Where the lines intersect, measure 6″ up and mark, then 6″ down and mark. Again, using the center, measure 4″ left and mark, then 4″ right and mark.

4. Make an oval by connecting the dots. Your opening should be 12″ high by 8″ wide.

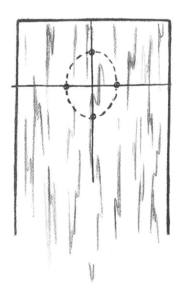

5. Drill a hole somewhere along the circumference of the oval. This hole should be large enough for your jigsaw blade.

6. Place your jigsaw blade in the starter hole and begin cutting along your oval outline. Again, this doesn't have to be perfect. You will be covering the edges with padding and vinyl.

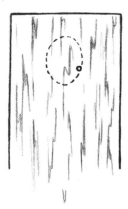

Cutting the Rabbet

1. Set your long rails on the same sturdy object on which you placed your plywood.

2. Measure 2″ from each end, and mark with a pencil.

3. Adjust your circular saw's blade depth to ¾″ deep and make a series of narrow parallel cuts, about ¼″ apart, from the end of the long rails up until you reach your 2″ mark.

4. Loosen the wood bits with a hammer.

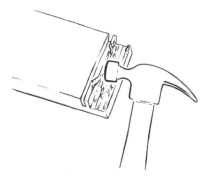

5. Use a chisel to clean out the remaining wood bits until you have as smooth a finish as possible.

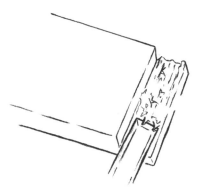

6. You now have a clean "rabbet," which you will need to construct tight joints and a sturdy table.

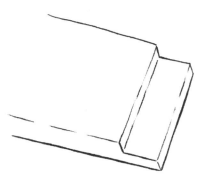

Getting Attached

You made it—you're done cutting. Now it's time to put the table together.

1. Attach the legs to the short rails, screwing two lag bolts into each leg.

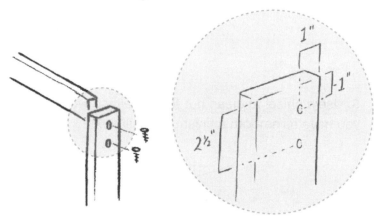

2. Now attach the long rails to complete your frame. Use two to four drywall screws per leg. For better support, drill in the drywall screws at a slight angle.

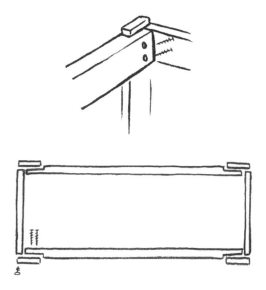

Putting on the Top

Now you'll want to attach the top of the massage table to the frame.

1. Take the plywood and place it on top of the frame. Double-check that it's centered. There should be about 1.5″ of overhang on all four sides.

2. Drill in drywall screws all around the table, as shown.

More Cushion for the Pushin'

At this point, you've successfully constructed a table with a gaping hole. You can either call it a day and be content with an extremely flawed dining room table, or you can add a little padding and turn it into an awesome, full-fledged massage table.

1. Lay your padding on top of the table.

2. With a pencil, trace the underside of the padding along the table edge. Don't forget to trace around the face hole as well.

3. Take out your razor blade and cut off the excess padding, using your pencil marks as a guide.

4. Glue your perfectly cut padding to the top of the table.

Vinyl Tap

Once the padding is in place, you're ready to add the vinyl.

1. Roll out the vinyl and center it atop the padding.

2. From the underside of the table, staple the vinyl into place starting with one of the corners. Then move to the next corner, pulling the vinyl taut and securing it with another staple. Continue moving to the two remaining corners, pulling the vinyl taut each time.

3. Once all of the corners have been secured, move around to each of the table sides, pulling the vinyl taut before stapling.

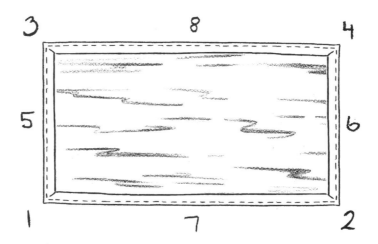

4. Complete a circumference of the table, securing the vinyl with a staple every couple of inches.

5. Using a single-edge razor, cut away the excess vinyl.

Finish with the Face Hole

1. Once you've securely stapled the vinyl to the underside of the table, it's time to wrap the vinyl around the face hole. Crawl under the table and poke a hole in the center of the circle.

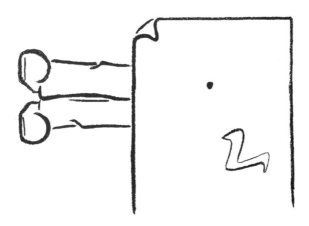

2. Crawl back out from under the table and find the hole you've just made.

3. Cut several straight lines with your razor. Leave about 2.25″ from the outside edge of your hole, as shown.

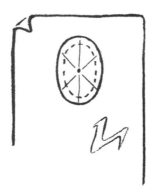

4. Crawl back under the table one last time and pull the vinyl taut. Staple it to the underside of the table.

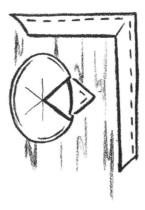

5. Admire the finished product.

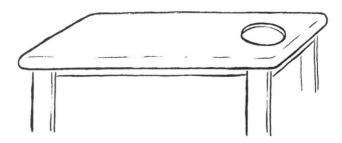

Construction

Copping a Feel

You could probably use a massage after putting together that massage table. Unfortunately, that's not how dating works. You still have to give the massage—and you actually have to do it well. With that in mind, here are a few massage moves proven to result in a happy ending.

1. The Golden Shoulder

Shoulders are home to several important muscles, which can result in more built-up tension than a road-trip with Angelina Jolie and Jennifer Aniston. Work your thumbs in with firm, alternating kneading motions until the only tension remaining is sexual in nature.

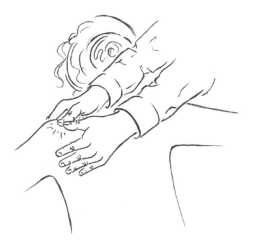

 View from a Broad

"I know it's a cliché, but women love a guy who's good with his hands. It shows he can get things done, that he's in control."

Tiffany, Roanoke, VA

Construction

233

2. Back to the Suture

Now move down to the small of her back. Dig in your fingers firmly but with tenderness, moving up the sides of her spine all the way to her neck. Avoid using your nails or, later, she'll use her teeth.

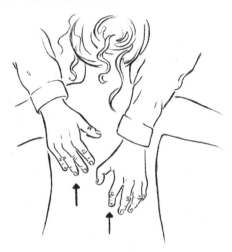

2. The TSA Pat-Down

Your date's Christmas hams should be treated just as you would treat any other region of her back, as this area is home to a plentitude of potentially tense muscle fibers. Just avoid being overtly sexual or invasive like the actual TSA, or else she'll never consent to a strip search.

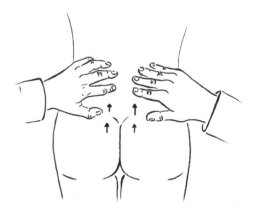

Magic

Not Quite Enough — Card Handling

Almost Enough — Deception

Just Enough — The Tricks

A Sure Thing — The Foolproof Date Proposal

*P*ulling off a badass illusion and getting laid aren't really that different. They both require deception, showmanship, and fast fingers. Both should leave your partner breathlessly wondering: "How did you do that?" Both usually conclude as three or four doves flutter into the room.

So it should come as no surprise that knowing a little magic can go a long way in the bedroom. And it can even help put girls there in the first place. Need proof? Consider the quality of women some of the more illustrious illusionists have brought in. In 1994 magician David Copperfield performed the most amazing magic trick of his life. He pulled Claudia Schiffer out of his ass and married her. Or how about David Blaine? Thanks to his gimmicky, self-aggrandizing TV specials, he's like the Tiger Woods of magic. And don't forget Harry Potter—he's tapping known firecrotch Ginny Weasley.

Of course, we shouldn't overstate our case. Women aren't exactly breaking down the door to the public library because your local magician is duping kids with Three-card Monte in the family learning annex. When it comes to magic, there seems to be a razor-thin line between "suave illusionist" and "creepy guy who's legally banned from living within 10 miles of an elementary school."

Don't worry. We'll help you straddle that line. And we'll help you use magic to get girls to straddle you.

It turns out that magic is a better icebreaker than the Titanic. You can penetrate the bulletproof defenses of the frostiest of sorority girls with five simple words: "Wanna see a cool trick?" And if she thinks it's part of the trick, she'll find herself willing to give up her name, her cell phone number, how many dates it takes to sleep with her (one)—anything that might help assist the illusion. Because girls love a mystery. No date has ever ended with a girl demanding: "Please take me home. I'm having far too magical a time tonight."

This all sounds wonderful, but you still need an act. Which is convenient because we've got one for you, and it's easy as hell to pull off. You won't need to figure out how to escape from a strait-jacket in order to escape another night of jacking it. We're merely going to teach you a handful of impressive, easy-to-learn tricks. They'll be all you really need to make a pair of girl's underwear magically disappear and reappear on your bedroom floor.

Magic

The Bare Necessities

A deck of cards, a coin, a beer bottle, magic fingers.

On Good Terms

Card Flourish: A feat performed with a deck of cards that is designed to demonstrate dexterity.

Corgi Shuffle: A basic shuffle where one spreads out a deck facedown and slides around the cards until they're fully mixed up.

Force: When a trick's participant believes he or she is controlling a particular outcome, but that outcome is actually being determined by the magician.

Not Quite Enough — Card Handling

The primary objective of magicians is to delight and impress. That's why they wear their fancy top hats and capes, and more often than not, a luxurious mustache. That's also why they pull a fluffy white rabbit out of their hat instead of a deceased, maggot-covered rat.

These flourishes offer no real utility other than giving off visual pheromones. They are also a great way to convey authority— and an ideal way to teach your fingers some dexterity, which could definitely be a big help later on in the night.

Card Flourishes

We're going to teach you a fan and a cut. As impressive as they might seem, they're ultimately pretty simple to learn. This means that not only will they require a mere modicum of patience, they're also kind of a perfect thing to teach your date. She deserves to learn something, after all, because you're not going to be able to teach her any of the tricks. That would be a clear violation of the magician's code, which states that you should never reveal the mechanics of a trick. And we're strong proponents of the magician's code—aside from the fact that we're going to shit all over it later on in this chapter.

Cuts

Cuts are designed to transpose two halves of a shuffled deck. Your basic cut is all well and good for the common man, but a magician will want something with a little more flair. These maneuvers take a little repetition, but for some cheap showmanship, they're totally worth it. Once you've figured out the steps involved, it's surprisingly enjoyable to practice your form while watching a movie or sitting in a classroom as your professor prattles on about nothing. And while it does take some time to familiarize yourself with the mechanics, much like in relationships, you won't need to be entirely present during the learning process.

Charlier Cut (pronounced shar-lee-ay)

1. Grip the deck in a raised mechanic's grip. Your pinkie and index fingers should be at the short ends of the deck, as shown.

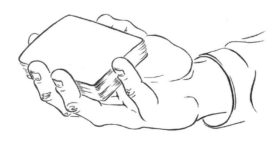

Magic

2. Using your index finger, drop the bottom half of the deck into your palm.

3. Still using your index finger, raise the dropped bottom half of the deck so that the two halves form a "T." As you're doing this, lift your thumb.

4. Continue pivoting the bottom half of the deck with your index finger until it's resting upright against your raised thumb. Let the top half drop into your palm, and then use your thumb to direct the bottom half on top of it. Now square it all up with your thumb and fingers.

Magic

VideoMark:
Charlier Cut

Fanning

It is possible—and highly majestic-looking—to evenly fan out a deck of cards in your hand in one quick, fluid motion. This can be a striking flourish to pull off, because once you've figured out the mechanics, you can spread out the cards at a ridiculous speed. A properly deployed fan will make it seem like you're working with a trick deck, or that you spent countless hours gluing cards together. Alternatively, a botched fan will make it seem like you spent countless hours sniffing glue—so make sure you've got the process nailed down.

Thumb Fan

1. Hold the deck in your left hand with your thumb in the front and your other four fingers gripping the back.

2. Now grip the front of the deck with your right hand. Place your index finger on the top, your thumb on the left side, and your other fingers on the right side.

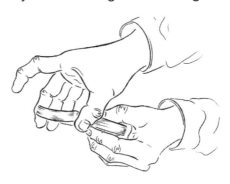

3. Maintain pressure on the deck with your thumb and fingers, and at the same time, use your other hand to move the deck from side to side to give it a clean bevel. This will help you make an even fan.

4. In one clean motion, turn your right hand clockwise and at the same time apply pressure with your left thumb so that the cards fan out evenly.

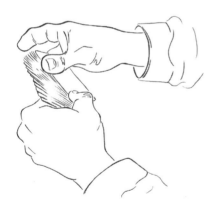

VideoMark:
Thumb Fan

Magic

Blue Balls Beware

Although it might seem like a fun idea, don't give yourself a special magician's stage name. If you do, no matter what it is, in her head she will hear it as "Chester the Amazing Molester."

Almost Enough — Deception

In the world of magic, there are no rules. Or at least it should seem that way to the audience. In fact, there're plenty of rules. You're still confined by the harsh world of physics and will therefore need to rely on the rules of deception—with which you're probably quite familiar. Deception is how most guys get laid in the first place. The deception used in magic is not that different. It merely requires a more thoughtful, structured approach than simply saying you enjoy volunteering your free time reading to slow children.

How to Mindfuck an Audience:
The Three Forms of Deception

Successful deception techniques draw attention away from the revealing mechanics of your trick while simultaneously drawing attention toward elements of the illusion. The various techniques can be distilled into three fundamental categories: movement, timing and verbal.

Movement

People are reflexively attracted toward movement. You can use this instinct to your advantage by controlling your audience's focus with movement. Where you're looking will also greatly impact where your audience looks. It's all about eye control. If you keep their attention directed where you want it, it's easier to obscure the secrets of your illusion.

Timing

The pace of your illusion should be structured in such a way that important details are obscured, while misleading details are emphasized.

Verbal

Verbal deception is a polite way to say that you should lie to your audience. You've probably used verbal deception in your personal life to skip out on a day of work, to sustain your drinking habit or to prolong an unhappy relationship. This fraudulence will serve you well in the world of magic.

French Drop

The French Drop is a basic sleight-of-hand trick involving the disappearance of a coin. It's not unlike the trick your grandfather might have attempted during your childhood when he pulled a coin out of your ear, or the trick your uncle played on you when he stole your pocket change to purchase alcohol. Either way, the mechanics of this trick are so simple that the illusion completely falls apart unless the magician utilizes all three elements of deception.

Magic

1. Hold a coin in one hand—let's say your right—with the tips of your fingers. Your thumb should be on the topside of the coin, which should be facing the audience.

2. Bring your left hand over to your right, as if to grab the coin. Your left thumb should be positioned behind the coin while your other fingers obscure the audience's view.

3. Allow the coin to gently fall back into your right palm by slightly raising your right thumb. At the same time, grip your left hand as if to clench the coin.

4. Turn your right hand and point to your left, as if indicating the location of the coin.

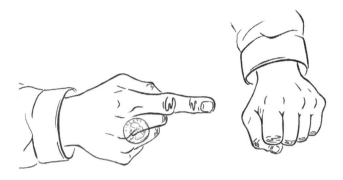

5. Dramatically open your left hand to reveal that the coin has mysteriously vanished.

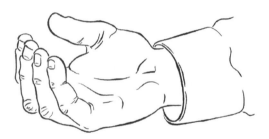

VideoMark:
The French Drop

Magic

Let's look at the multitude of misdirection going down:

Movement: Clenching your left fist is a simple but effective way to communicate that you're hiding the coin in that hand. This act is an example of a superfluous movement that distracts the audience. Similarly, your own eyes should be focused on this left hand, inviting your audience to follow suit.

Note: Your right hand should also be resting naturally at your side. All the movement should be taking place away from the actual location of the coin.

Timing: If you perform the French Drop in one quick, fluid motion, the audience may not have enough time to think through where the coin actually is. Practiced magicians can perform sleights of hand like this at speeds that cannot be followed with the naked eye. Ideally, your audience won't even remember where they saw the coin last.

Take time to make the coin "disappear." If you reveal that your left hand is empty prematurely, your audience may conclude that it never left your right hand. Instead, keep them absorbed in the false drama of how you're going to remove the coin from your left hand.

Verbal: As you "take" the coin with your left hand, bolster the illusion by talking your audience through the trick: "Now here's the coin in my right hand. I'm just going to take it with my left and secure it tightly." The first sentence is accurate and invites your audience to trust your narrative; the second is perjury. But your audience will have an easier time believing the part they can't see if you're shown to be honest where they actually can see it.

Magic

Using all of these elements simultaneously, the simple act of dropping a coin into your fingers and clenching your fist over a pocket of air can become a divine act of magic.

Dropping Knowledge

Magic comes from the word magi, a priestly self in the ancient religion of Zoroastrianism. Magi relied on astrology, which was then regarded as a science. As astrology became associated with the occult, so too did the term magi. Thus, magic came to refer to any dealings in supernatural forces.

Just Enough — The Tricks

The meat and potatoes of magic, of course, are the tricks. Without tricks, a magician is just a deceitful fruitcake in a top hat. With them, he is a crowd-pleasing miracle worker with innumerable secrets. We've included three effective illusions that build off the principles of misdirection. They're ideal to pull off in a bar or party setting—i.e., crowded places where one might try to impress a girl—and they give you an immediate advantage over non-magical dudes whose only "trick" involves the ability to get sloppily drunk and navigate the folds of overweight girls.

Magic

The only caution we suggest is that you familiarize yourself with the trick's mechanics beforehand. Practice on your friends and your family. These aren't difficult tricks, but if you seem like you're not 100 percent sure what you're doing, the illusion crumbles under the weight of your uncertainty.

Just the Tip

The most important element you'll need when demonstrating your magic trick is confidence. Even if some disaster befalls your performance, if you remain in control and act like you meant for it to happen, you can almost always figure out a way to save the illusion. So don't perform a trick for a girl if you feel hazy on the mechanics. It's better to know one trick backward and foward than a hundred tricks inadequately.

Wingman in the Wings

Ideal places to perform the trick: bar, wedding reception, AA meeting

What you need: any five (or so) random objects, a trustworthy friend, one drink

This trick relies on a little covert assistance from your friend. As a reward for his participation, you'll pay for the drink he'll need in order to pull off this trick—and if he's lucky, he'll get to bring home whatever repulsive hambeast your girl brought with her to the bar.

The Trick: Tell an attractive coed that she's emanating a powerful aura—so strong, in fact, that any object she touches would leave a psychic imprint. Prove this by leaving the area to buy her a drink while she touches one of a series of random objects. When you return, you'll be able to sense exactly which one it was.

The Performance:

1. Beforehand, you and your friend will make a secret agreement. When you inspect the particular object that was touched, he'll casually take a sip from his drink.

2. After explaining to the girl that you possess a powerful awareness of psychic energy, arrange five or so random objects on the table. These can be coasters, drink glasses, a napkin, etc. If you want to get more personal, use objects from her own purse (sunglasses, cell phone, birth control pills, etc.). Say that you're going to leave the area to buy her a drink and ask her to touch one of the items at random in your absence.

3. Leave the room and actually purchase the drink (this helps your cause regardless of the magic trick). When you return, closely examine each of the objects in a meditative, metaphysically inquisitive way. Turn them over in your hand as if appealing to some unknown psychic power. Meanwhile, discreetly keep an eye on your wingman. As instructed, he should casually sip his drink when your hand touches the pertinent object.

4. Even after your friend has indicated the object in question, continue to examine the remaining articles. Showmanship is always central when selling an illusion. You could, for example, key in on one of the objects she didn't touch—but then, at the last moment, dramatically shift to the correct one. Be sure to talk aloud through the process (verbal misdirection). Describe the correct object as being warm or emanating an unusual energy.

5. Now reveal the object, much to the girl's admiration and excitement.

As with many illusions, the secret to this trick is the most obvious one imaginable: You're able to determine her object because a third party was present when she selected it. To avoid letting her come to this conclusion, the principles of misdirection should be in full effect. This trick is a great introduction to applying these principles, because the basic mechanics of the illusion are almost impossible to botch. There's no sleight of hand, no need to keep track of a card. All you need is a willing friend and a cheap drink.

Blue Balls Beware

Because you're relying on your friend, this trick is vulnerable to failing through no fault of your own. If your friend takes multiple sips or none at all, he is probably an alcoholic or an asshole. According to a longstanding magician's bylaw, at this point you are justified in sleeping with his girlfriend or mother.

Tear Force One

Ideal places to perform the trick: dorm room, bar, house party, women's prison

What you need: index card-sized piece of paper, pen

This is a classic bit of street magic that can arouse some intense reactions, which makes it a great way to flirt with strangers. And it's pretty obvious that the whole point of "street magic" is for magicians to get laid in the middle of the day.

Magic

The Trick: Prompt your participant to write down a name only she could possibly know—the more emotional, the better. Ideally, her grandmother just passed away. That might sound cruel, but Maw-Maw lived a long life and her death would really be a convenient asset for this trick. Next, without peeking, you'll rip up the paper and hand her the pieces. After a few tense moments, you'll "read her mind" and conjure up the answer. And she'll be overwhelmed with emotion. Take her back home for a little consolation.

The Performance:

1. Prior to performing the trick, procure a piece of paper roughly the size of an index card—you don't have to be exact about the size so it doesn't matter as long as it's squarish and capable of being torn.

2. Now ask the girl to think of a name. You'll probably want to ask her for a loved one's name, but it could also be her favorite high school teacher to whom she lost her virginity to. (Hopefully those aren't the same person.) Prompting her to provide a more personal name is recommended if you want maximum emotional impact— i.e., "Think of a loved one who's passed away."

Magic

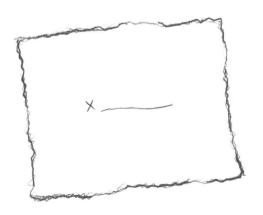

3. In the very center of the paper, draw an "X" followed by a blank line, as in a signature line. It's important to place this line in the middle of the paper.

4. Ask the girl to write down the word on the line you provided. Make a point to turn away while she writes. Don't let her think you're peeking.

5. When she's finished, take the paper and fold it twice, with her writing on the inside of the fold. Make sure to fold it from top to bottom, and then from left to right. Do not fold it twice in the same direction.

6. Now it's time to tear up the paper. And here's the trick: The upper left corner where there are no exposed edges (where the solid edges meet) is the location of the center portion of the paper. This is where the name is written. You'll want to tear the paper vertically down the center first and then stack the pieces so that the information is on the bottom of the stack. Next, tear the pieces horizontally across the center, once again keeping the valuable corner intact in the very back.

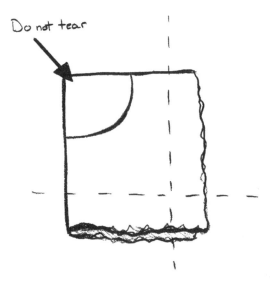

7. Using your thumb, discreetly slide the important torn piece into one of your palms. You can do this while continuing to tear the remaining bits so that the motion doesn't seem obvious.

8. After you've finished tearing the paper into sufficiently small pieces, put the scraps into the girl's hand and ask her to clench her fist around the pieces. Ask her to once again concentrate on what she's written. Appear to focus on reading her mind.

9. The easiest way to take a peek at the scrap of paper tucked into your palm is to close your eyes and pretend to focus on psychically determining the name she's written down. With your eyes slanted downward, you should be able to take a quick glance into your hand. She won't suspect what you're doing because she thinks she has all the paper bits in her hands. This is also a good opportunity to check out her boobs.

Magic

10. Deliver her the goods. After having prolonged the tension, say aloud the name she's written on the paper. Alternately, you could write the name on a fresh piece of paper—a convenient way to look at the scrap of paper still in your hand.

The emotional weight of this trick can be pretty powerful thanks to the personal significance of what the girl has written down. If done with conviction and poise, the result will be a girl whose emotions are torn apart more thoroughly than the paper used for the trick. All you need to do is pick up the pieces.

VideoMark:
Tear Force One

66 99
Quintessential Quotation

Michael Bluth: So this is the magic trick, huh?

'Gob' Bluth: Illusion, Michael. A trick is something a whore does for money.

—Arrested Development

Magic

The Easy ESP Card Trick

Ideal places to perform the trick: your apartment, restaurant, Tupperware party

What you need: a deck of cards, her favorite booze

Most regular card tricks center on the same tired song and dance of magicians magically determining some particular playing card. Even when successfully performed, the process is dull because the climax is always the same: "Is this your card?" The Easy ESP Card Trick steps up the stakes by allowing the magical card-finding to be performed by your audience. This active participation makes it the perfect card trick to perform for a girl. Oh, and it's blindingly easy to pull off.

The Trick: You'll shuffle up a deck using the **corgi shuffle** (also known as the beginner's shuffle)—spread out all the cards facedown and mix them up with your hands. Next you'll ask the girl to gather up her psychic powers and locate a certain seemingly random card. You will pick the card she chose without showing her, and then ask her to locate a second card in the same fashion. Now complete the trick by psychically locating a card of your own. When she's prepared to be blown away, reveal the three cards in your hand; magically, they're the three very cards you asked for. Now it's your turn to prepare to be blown.

The Performance:

1. While explaining to the girl that you're going to test her powers of ESP, shuffle a deck of cards. (This is a good opportunity to utilize those flourishes and cuts described in the Not Quite Enough section.) When you're finished, discreetly look at the bottom card and make note of it. In this example, let's say the card is the ace of hearts.

2. Spread the cards out on the table and mix them up using the corgi shuffle—but keep track of the ace of hearts. Do this by discreetly keeping your thumb on the card as you mix up the deck.

3. Tell the girl to concentrate and to use her psychic abilities to pick out the ace of hearts. Make it seem as though this were just a random card that popped into your head— "Okay, let's see . . . I don't know, let's go with the ace of hearts." Tell her to really visualize the card. Now have her point to where she thinks the card is located. She'll manage to fuck it up, of course—she's not really psychic. Without showing her the card, pick it up and look at it, saying something along the lines of, "Hmm. Very interesting." Let's say the card she actually managed to pick up is the two of diamonds.

4. Ask her to pick out a second card, this time requesting the two of diamonds she just picked out. Again, make it

seem like you're asking for an arbitrary card. She'll pick out another random card (let's say it's the ten of clubs). Again, take a look at it and say something mysterious like, "Ah. You've clearly had experience working psychic energy before."

5. Now tell her you'll pick out a card. Once again making it seem like a random card, announce that you'll pick out the two of diamonds. Since you already have this card in your hands, the actual card you're going to pick up is the ace of hearts you've been tracking—and the card you originally asked her to pick up.

In your hands you now have the three cards.

6. Ask her if she remembers which cards you wanted her to pick out. Take a moment to build the tension and then lay the three cards on the table one by one. She'll probably freak out, or at least wonder aloud how you managed to find the cards. Simply tell her that apparently both of you are psychic, and that you should get a motel room to celebrate.

This trick is the perfect combination of difficult to figure out and difficult to fuck up. Now that you've been told how it works, it probably seems pretty obvious. It's not. Her guess will probably be that the trick involved some sort of sleight of hand. Let her think so—that's giving you far more credit then you deserve.

Magic

There is one wrinkle: Suppose one of the cards she picks out is that bottom card you tracked. Perfect—the trick is over. You don't even need to pick out a card yourself because you'll have everything you need in your hands. If the very first card she happens to pick up is your card (a one in 52 chance), there'll be no deceit involved whatsoever.

You can just flip over the card and stop there. Although, in this scenario it may be a good idea to flip over the table entirely and run away because it's possible she actually is psychic. And anybody who can read your thoughts would probably try to have you arrested.

A Sure Thing —The Foolproof Date Proposal

Magic

The Foolproof Date Proposal

Ideal places to perform the trick: crowded bar, raucous party, strip club, Canada

What you need: napkin, pen

Not every magic trick is meant to amaze your audience. Oh, this one will do that too—but its real goal is to set you up on a date with a girl you don't know. It can be performed anywhere one might mingle with girls. Needless to say, alcohol provides its own sort of misdirection—which means less work for you and a greater chance that your illusion will be successful.

The Setup: You'll approach a desirable girl and tell her you can predict the future. Ask for her phone number, so you can text her a demonstration of your talents. Send the text—but tell her not to look at it yet. Next, you'll take a piece of paper and tear it into six pieces. On one side you will write six days of the week (leaving out Sunday), and on the other side, six types of food (Italian, French, etc.). Through a process of elimination, she'll end up choosing a day of the week and a food type. Now she can look at the text you already sent: It's a picture of you holding a sign asking for a date. But the sign will include the day of the week and the food type she just picked. She'll drop her jaw, and you'll be rewarded with a date. And if you're lucky, she'll drop her jaw once more.

The Performance:

1. Prior to going out, determine the date you want. Decide both the day of the week and the type of food. Use basic date logic: Nobody goes out for dates on Sunday, whereas Thursday is usually pretty safe (it's more or less the weekend, but she's more likely to be free). Most girls like Italian food, but there may be some other cuisine in your area that's universally appealing. It's really up to you. In this particular example, let's assume you go with Thursday night and Italian food.

Magic

2. Write neatly on a piece of paper a note with your name and the phrase: "See you Thursday night for some Italian!" No little hearts or doilies.

3. Take a picture of the note and save it in your phone.

4. Now you're out and about. Drinks are being drunk and everyone's having a good time. Approach an attractive girl and see if there's any chemistry. This means that when you say hello, she doesn't immediately reach for her pepper spray.

5. Tell her you can predict the future. Ask for her number and send her the photo you previously saved to your phone. (If you're lazy, a plain text message works as an alternative.) Tell her not to look at the text just yet.

6. Grab a napkin or piece of paper and divide it into six pieces. On one side of each piece, write down six days of the week (skipping Sunday); on the other side, write down six food options (i.e., Italian, Chinese, Greek, sushi, Mexican, Middle Eastern, etc.). It doesn't matter which food option is written on the back of which day of the week.

Magic

7. Here comes the trick. You're going to take turns eliminating first food options, and then days of the week, until you're left with one of each. The elimination process is as follows: You must go first. Say, "I'm going to point to two options and you're going to choose which one of those to eliminate." Never point to the day of the week or food type you wrote on your cell phone sign.

You've eliminated one of the six options. Now it's her turn. Say, "Now you point to two options and I'll eliminate one." If one of her choices happens to coincide with the day of the week or food type written on your sign, simply eliminate the alternate option.

Do this back and forth until there are only two choices remaining. It will be her turn.

Because there are only two options left, she is in danger of eliminating the correct choice. So don't ask her to eliminate one this time. Instead, ask her to simply pick up one of the remaining pieces of paper. If she picks up the option matching your text message picture, say, "Okay, great. We'll go with that." If she picks up the other option, say, "Okay, good. Now move that to the elimination pile."

In other words, she doesn't know whether she's eliminating the options she picks up or selecting it as her final choice—it's actually your decision. In magician's parlance, this is called a force.

8. Now that you've determined the choice of food, flip over the pieces of paper so that the days of the week are visible. Repeat the elimination process, using the same technique to lead her into choosing whichever day you wrote on your cell phone sign.

Now that she's made her "decisions," show her your text. Nice one, Nostradamus: You've predicted the future.

Making a girl think she's come to a decision that you've secretly implanted in her brain is a valuable skill even outside the realm of magic. In many ways, the most miraculous "trick" of all is convincing a girl she wants to see you naked. She doesn't, of course—nobody does. But with enough misdirection, almost anything's possible.

Magic

Acknowledgments

We want to thank our wives Amy Emmett & Danielle DeAngelo
for not divorcing us in our pursuit to help men everywhere get laid.
Although, if they ever do decide to divorce us we are confident
the material covered in this book will keep us getting laid.

Thanks to our parents Nancy and Jim DeAngelo and Jane and
Collin Emmett for their support in writing a book about getting laid.
We hope you will proudly display this on your coffee tables, the
coffee tables we were conceived on.

Special Thanks to Lee Seidenberg.

Contributors:	Eric Karjala
Additional material by:	Paul Watcher
	Sam Zayvan
	Eric Immerman
	Jonathan Stokes
Illustrator:	Kendra Malcolm
Design:	Renee Lee
Experts:	Guitar—JSchem
	Magic—Dan White
	Cooking—Matt Brehony
	Wine—Matt Brehony
	French—Gaston
	Religion—Frank Podesta
	Construction—Rhys Mathews
	Roger Binns
	Danielle DeAngelo
	Astronomy—Jonathan Poppele

About The Authors

Tyler DeAngelo and Brad Emmett are creative directors at a prominent, award-winning New York advertising agency. They have each successfully employed their own teachings and managed to marry Radio City Rockettes.